THE 100+ SERIES™

GRAMMAR

Essential Practice for Key Grammar Topics

Grades 3-4

D1451813

Carson-Dellosa Publishing LLC
Greensboro, North Carolina

Credits

Content Editor: Christine Schwab

Visit *carsondellosa.com* for correlations to Common Core, state, national, and Canadian provincial standards.

Carson-Dellosa Publishing LLC
PO Box 35665
Greensboro, NC 27425 USA
carsondellosa.com

ISBN 978-1-4838-1556-5
05-344187784

Table of Contents

Common Core Alignment Chart

Common Core State Standard*		Practice Page(s)
Language Standards		
Conventions of Standard English	3.L.1–3.L.2	15–28, 31–96, 99–110, 113–120
Knowledge of Language	3.L.3	24, 33, 34, 37, 45, 70, 77, 86, 112
Vocabulary Acquisition and Use	3.L.4–3.L.6	9–14
Conventions of Standard English	4.L.1–4.L.2	15–40, 62–66, 70, 71, 97, 98, 104, 105, 113–120
Knowledge of Language	4.L.3	24, 33, 34, 36–40, 45, 70, 77, 86, 111, 112
Vocabulary Acquisition and Use	4.L.4–4.L.6	5–8, 12–14

Introduction

Good grammar skills are essential for effective writing and communication. Organized by specific grammar rules, this book will enhance students' knowledge and usage of proper grammar. These skills include the basic parts of speech, sentence components, vocabulary, and other conventions of Standard English.

The grade-appropriate exercises in this series will strengthen any language arts program. Students will practice and review various grammar skills and concepts throughout the book through activities that align to the Common Core State Standards in English language arts. The standards and corresponding pages are listed in Common Core Alignment Chart above. Use this chart to plan your instruction, for skill practice, or for remediation of a specific standard.

Synonyms

Synonyms are words that have the same or nearly the same meaning.

last, final   mistake, error

Write the word in the parentheses ( ) that means the same as the word on the left.

Synonyms

1. small   _____   (large, little, round)

2. close   _____   (easy, far, near)

3. sad   _____   (unhappy, glad, nice)

4. bright   _____   (dull, brilliant, clean)

5. false   _____   (clear, true, wrong)

6. large   _____   (little, lamp, big)

7. gift   _____   (gem, present, store)

8. fast   _____   (fresh, tame, quick)

9. tidy   _____   (neat, seed, near)

10. stone   _____   (store, rock, circle)

11. fat   _____   (tall, square, plump)

12. raise   _____   (lower, lift, carry)

Synonyms

Select a synonym for the underlined word in each sentence from the words in the word bank. Write the synonym.

Word Bank

arrive	error	large	mix	over	price	put
reduce	robber	scared	sick	small	talk	under

1. The dog sat <u>below</u> the chair. _____

2. Tony <u>placed</u> his book on the table. _____

3. The <u>big</u> animal was in a cage. _____

4. The <u>burglar</u> stole a lot of money. _____

5. The clock was <u>above</u> the desk. _____

6. The loud noise <u>frightened</u> the baby. _____

7. I made a <u>mistake</u> on my test. _____

8. The <u>cost</u> was $1.00 for the notebook. _____

9. The child became <u>ill</u> at school. _____

10. I ordered a <u>little</u> pizza. _____

11. Please <u>come</u> to my party at 7:00 pm. _____

12. Will you <u>speak</u> to the class? _____

13. Dad needs to <u>lessen</u> his work load. _____

14. You need to <u>blend</u> the eggs and sugar. _____

Antonyms

Antonyms are words that have opposite meanings.

north   south

Select an antonym for the underlined word in each sentence from the words in the word bank. Write the antonym.

Word Bank

ancient	assemble	cooked	day	disarray	evil	increase
learned	minor	praised	present	purchase	sharp	strong	unbolt

1. The old man was <u>feeble</u>. _____

2. The castle was <u>modern</u> inside. _____

3. Caroline likes <u>raw</u> carrots. _____

4. The character in the book was <u>good</u>. _____

5. She <u>taught</u> Spanish every day. _____

6. Drew was <u>absent</u> yesterday. _____

7. The knife was <u>dull</u> and rusty. _____

8. The teacher <u>criticized</u> the student. _____

9. <u>Lock</u> the door, please. _____

10. The meeting will <u>adjourn</u> soon. _____

11. It was a <u>major</u> decision. _____

12. I am going to <u>sell</u> shoes. _____

13. You should <u>decrease</u> your sugar intake. _____

14. We went fishing in the middle of the <u>night</u>. _____

15. The room was in great <u>order</u>. _____

Synonyms and Antonyms: Review

Write a synonym and an antonym for each key word.

Synonym	Key Word	Antonym	in inside out
_____	whole	_____	
_____	quick	_____	
_____	stay	_____	
_____	small	_____	
_____	near	_____	
_____	loud	_____	
_____	glad	_____	
_____	dirty	_____	
_____	difficult	_____	
_____	wet	_____	
_____	same	_____	
_____	ill	_____	
_____	repair	_____	
_____	finish	_____	
_____	depart	_____	
_____	begin	_____	
_____	high	_____	
_____	large	_____	
_____	shut	_____	
_____	kind	_____	
_____	smart	_____	

Homonyms

Homonyms are words that are pronounced the same but have different meanings and spellings.

tow   toe

Read the homonyms. Choose the correct homonym to complete each sentence.

(two, to)

1. We have _____ apple pies.

   We went _____ the store.

(pear, pair, pare)

2. I ate the delicious _____ .

   I have a _____ of gloves.

   Will you _____ the peaches?

(sun, son)

3. They have a _____ and a daughter.

   The _____ is shining today.

(ate, eight)

4. I _____ a pizza for lunch.

   I bought _____ pencils.

(red, read)

5. I _____ the book.

   My book is _____ .

(one, won)

6. I _____ the race.

   I have _____ brother.

Homonyms

Circle the correct homonym.

1. We went (to, too, two) the store.

2. The pig's (tale, tail) was short.

3. The (knight, night) rode a beautiful horse.

4. I have a (soar, sore) on my knee.

5. Mother said, "Please do not (waste, waist) time."

6. We had rare (steak, stake) for dinner.

7. We can (beet, beat) your team playing baseball.

8. Did you (rap, wrap) the present?

9. Do not run down the (stairs, stares).

10. Let's (paws, pause) for a drink of water.

11. Are you going to (wait, weight) for me?

12. I'm taking a (course, coarse) in English.

13. Have you (scene, seen) my science book?

14. The (sum, some) of the problem is 10.

15. Which soda did you (chews, choose)?

16. May I have a (piece, peace) of cake?

17. I have sand in my (pale, pail).

18. Please come to (hour, our) house.

19. My (aunt, ant) and uncle took us to the park.

20. Did you tie a square (not, knot)?

Homonyms

Each silly sentence has four homonyms. Rewrite each sentence using the correct words.

1. I wood like the hole peace of stake.

   _____

2. Isle where my blew genes tomorrow.

   _____

3. Hour male is knot do to be delivered today.

   _____

4. Last knight, we one for sense.

   _____

5. Inn to daze we go on our crews.

   _____

6. Next weak, my ant mite come hear.

   _____

7. My sun will by knew close.

   _____

8. The knew plain that flu bye was noisy.

   _____

9. Ewe weight write near the gait.

   _____

10. Eye sea my deer friend nose you.

    _____

Prefixes

A **prefix** is a word part that is added to the beginning of a word to change the meaning of that word. Prefixes have meaning. Some prefixes may mean the same thing.

re- to do again	re + place = replace (to place again)
un- not	un + even = uneven (not even)
mid- middle	mid + air = midair (in the middle of the air)
in- not	in + dependent = independent (not dependent)

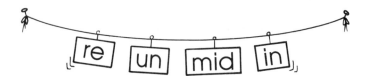

Use one of the four prefixes with each underlined word to write a new word that means the same as the description.

1. <u>paint</u> again   _____

2. not <u>fair</u>   _____

3. not <u>complete</u>   _____

4. <u>mount</u> again   _____

5. not <u>touched</u>   _____

6. <u>wind</u> again   _____

7. not <u>clear</u>   _____

8. <u>do</u> again   _____

9. not <u>direct</u>   _____

10. not <u>fit</u>   _____

11. in the middle of the <u>day</u>   _____

Name_____

Suffixes

A **suffix** is a word part that is added to the end of a word to change the meaning of that word. Suffixes have meaning. Some suffixes may mean more than one thing.

-er more than	high + er = higher (more high)
-er one who	sing + er = singer (one who sings)
-less without	fear + less = fearless (without fear)
-ful full of	fear + ful = fearful (full of fear)

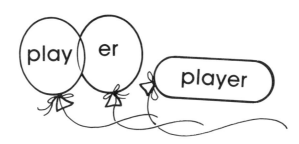

Use one of the three suffixes with each underlined word to write a new word that means the same as the description.

1. full of <u>wonder</u>   _____

2. without <u>hope</u>   _____

3. full of <u>grace</u>   _____

4. without <u>worth</u>   _____

5. one who can <u>clean</u>   _____

6. full of <u>success</u>   _____

7. without <u>use</u>   _____

8. one who can <u>read</u>   _____

9. without <u>help</u>   _____

10. one who can <u>teach</u>   _____

11. full of <u>cheer</u>   _____

Prefixes and Suffixes: Review

In each sentence, find a word with a prefix or a suffix. Circle the root word. Draw a line under the prefix or the suffix.

1. Every sentence should be meaningful.

2. Do not be careless about your clothes.

3. I need to redo my report.

4. The grizzly bear gave a frightful roar.

5. My misfortune was his gain.

6. The gardener will plant seeds in May.

7. The recipe said to precook the meat.

8. Did you unlock your suitcase?

9. In our city, the weather is changeable.

10. Wendy will start preschool in September.

11. Andre has a collection of wooden soldiers.

12. We live midway between New York and Boston.

13. My grandparents are inactive.

14. The painter will need a ladder for the ceiling.

15. Make the check payable to Dr. Walker.

16. My new kitchen chairs are uncomfortable

17. The table had a washable surface.

18. I think I'm predestined to teach school.

19. That newspaper reporter is hotheaded!

20. The trapeze artist did seem to be fearless.

Capital Letters

Use a capital letter for the first word of every sentence.

Vacations are fun.

Use a word from the word bank to complete each sentence.

Word Bank

airplanes	apples	blue	clowns	coats	do
dogs	pair	presents	seven	snow	trains

1. _____ are my favorite animals.

2. _____ days are in a week.

3. _____ are round and red.

4. _____ run on tracks.

5. _____ fly in the sky.

6. _____ is the color of the sky.

7. _____ means to have two.

8. _____ you have any brothers?

9. _____ make me laugh.

10. _____ falls in winter.

11. _____ keep us warm.

12. _____ are fun to open.

Capital Letters

Use capital letters for names of people and pets. Use a capital letter to begin each word in a name.

Steven Alvin Jung	Bandit
Lisa Maria Hagen	Mittens

Rewrite each name. Use capital letters where needed.

1. jan ellen shaw _____

2. mable mouse _____

3. paul mark conti _____

4. maria kaylen foster _____

5. rover _____

6. david joseph marino _____

7. nadia lin _____

8. chang lee _____

9. kenny david vale _____

10. thad edgar taylor _____

11. spot _____

12. jai ivey patel _____

13. ebony grace freeman _____

14. tabby _____

Capital Letters

Use a capital letter for a title in a name. Use a period after the abbreviation.

Mr. Sam Unger   Dr. Ella Irene Becker

Use a capital letter for an initial in a name. Use a period after the initial.

Tony L. Conti   Jill C. Dolby

Rewrite each sentence. Use capital letters and periods where needed.

1. mr jack m king is my friend.

   _____

2. dr robert e lewis is my doctor.

   _____

3. mrs ana s sanchez is my mother.

   _____

4. mia gave me a coloring book.

   _____

5. george washington was our first president.

   _____

6. kahla's dad is mr mario p silva.

   _____

7. my teacher is mr vincent r walker.

   _____

Capital Letters

Capitalize
- the first word of a sentence. (It is snowing.)
- names of people and pets. (Samia, Pluto)
- titles and abbreviations. (Miss Huber, Dr.)
- names of places and things. (Symphony Hall, Freedom Trail)
- the word I. (I am reading.)

Rewrite each sentence. Use capital letters where needed.

1. lisa and tripp went to see dr. upton yi.

   _____

2. i live on the corner of belt ave. and boise dr.

   _____

3. my dog's name is pancake.

   _____

4. did you watch nick at nite last night?

   _____

5. mr. perez works at the metropolitan museum.

   _____

6. i got presents for aunt emily and uncle jaime.

   _____

7. chandra and i went to the lincoln memorial.

   _____

8. the st. louis cardinals will be in the play-offs.

   _____

Capital Letters

Use capital letters for names of months, special days, and holiday. Look at the example on the calendar.

January			
New Year's Day 1.	2.	3.	4.
5.	6.	7.	8.
9.	10.	11.	12.

Rewrite each month, special day, and holiday on the calendar in order. Use capital letters.

1. january—new year's day martin luther king jr. day

2. february—valentine's day

3. march—st. patrick's day

4. april—april fool's day easter

5. may—memorial day mother's day

6. june—flag day father's day

7. july—independence day

8. august—friendship day

9. september—labor day

10. october—columbus day united nations day

11. november—thanksgiving veteran's day

12. december—christmas hanukkah

Capital Letters

Capitalize
- cities, states, and countries. (Tulsa, Oklahoma, United States)
- lakes, rivers, and oceans. (Blue River, Indian Ocean)
- holidays. (Thanksgiving)
- days of the week and months. (Monday, June)
- names for people of particular countries. (French)

Rewrite each sentence. Use capital letters.

1. The mississippi river is east of st. louis, missouri.

   _____

2. Many spanish people live in houston, texas.

   _____

3. Valentine's day is celebrated february 14.

   _____

4. School starts the first tuesday after labor day.

   _____

5. I swam in lake michigan when I was in chicago, illinois.

   _____

6. I visited london, england, last july.

   _____

7. hoover dam and lake mead are near las vegas.

   _____

8. Last monday, august 17, was my birthday.

   _____

Capital Letters

Use capital letters for most words in a book title. Always capitalize the first word and the last word. Do not capitalize some small words such as *the, in, to,* and *at*.

The Fox and the Hound

Write each book title on a book. Use capital letters where needed.

the egg and i   goldilocks and the three bears

railroads of the world   the story of george washington

cinderella   alice in wonderland

cat in the hat   how to write reports

jack and the beanstalk   jokes and riddles

Capital Letters

Use capital letters for titles of TV programs, movies, books, and poems. Do not capitalize some small words such as *and, of, in,* and *the*. Always capitalize the first and last words.

Flying to the Moon

Rewrite the title below the book, TV screen, or movie screen. Use capital letters where needed.

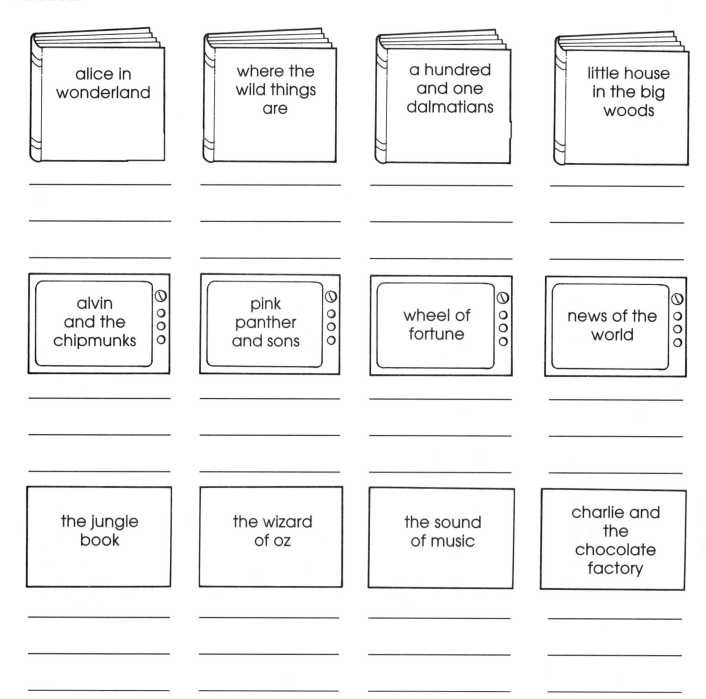

Capital Letters

Capitalize
- the first word of a direct quotation. ("Can you play?" asked Jan.)
- the first word in a greeting of a letter. (Dear Neil,)
- The first word in the closing of a letter. (Your friend, Tracy)

Rewrite each sentence. Use capital letters where needed.

1. Dad said, "brady, let's play ball."

   _____

2. The teacher asked, "have you finished your homework?"

   _____

3. My note ended, "your friend, nina."

   _____

4. "that's it," said Sean. "that's the right answer."

   _____

5. Mother's note to my teacher began, "dear miss beck."

   _____

6. "i got a new bike!" yelled Erik.

   _____

7. The thank-you note ended, "gratefully yours, mrs. sabatino."

   _____

8. I whispered, "be quiet; the baby is sleeping."

   _____

Capital Letters: Review

All about Me

Complete each sentence using capital letters and periods where needed.

1. My name is _____

2. The date I was born is _____

3. I live in the city of _____ ,

   in the state of _____ ,

   and in the country of _____

4. My favorite book is _____

5. My favorite holiday is _____

6. My favorite pet's name is _____

7. My favorite movie is _____

8. One of my best friends is _____

9. My favorite teacher is _____

10. My favorite day of the week is _____ because

    _____

11. My favorite song is _____

12. The names of my family members are:

    _____   _____   _____

    _____   _____   _____

Capital Letters: Review

In each sentence, circle the words that should begin with capital letters.

1. "after lunch," said sally, "let's go shopping."

2. i learned a lot from the book *inside the personal computer.*

3. my class from hudson school went to forest park.

4. carlos speaks spanish, french, and english.

5. the chung family lives on terrace drive.

6. "the new kid on the block" is a great story.

7. we saw the movie *ghostbusters* last saturday.

8. christopher columbus discovered america in 1492.

9. i was born june 12, 1965, in denver, colorado.

10. next thursday, mr. and mrs. espinosa have an anniversary.

11. my brother will attend harvard college in boston.

12. the letter to mason ended, "love from, aunt rose."

13. in hawaii, kamehameha day is celebrated each june.

14. mrs. friedman said, "don't be late for the party."

15. stone brothers hardware is on elm street.

Sentences

A **sentence** is a group of words that tells a complete idea.

The dictionaries are on the bottom shelf.

Not all groups of words are sentences. This group of words does not tell a complete idea.

The dictionaries on the bottom shelf

If the group of words below tells a complete idea, write **S** for *sentence*. If it does not tell a complete idea, write **NS** for *not a sentence*. Add a period if the group of words is a sentence.

1. _____   Cara ate her dinner

2. _____   After the ballgame

3. _____   The grass is green

4. _____   The English test tomorrow

5. _____   Because the dog

6. _____   The blue sweater in my drawer

7. _____   It is snowing

8. _____   Matt and Jimmy are twins

9. _____   Under the desk, my cat

10. _____   Drew visited Mexico

11. _____   The puzzle on the table

12. _____   Jayla dressed her doll

Sentences

A **sentence** must answer two questions.

Who or what did something? What happened?

Robert forgot his lunch.

Not all groups of words are sentences.

Forgot his lunch

After each group of words write **S** for *sentence* or **NS** for *not a sentence*. Add a period if it is a sentence.

1. The largest tigers in the world _____

2. We will visit Mexico _____

3. The present was wrapped _____

4. Amira swam very fast _____

5. A very funny comic book _____

6. Found and buried the nut _____

7. They ride horses _____

8. A speedboat on the lake _____

9. On Saturday, around the house _____

10. That joke was not funny _____

11. Lost her favorite ring at the store _____

12. During the Middle Ages, Robin Hood _____

13. Finally finished the job _____

14. The rocket landed yesterday _____

15. The tiny baby lying quietly in the cradle _____

Sentences

Rewrite the words in the correct order to make a complete sentence. Add a period where needed.

1. squirrel tree the gray our in little lives

   _____

2. a in tied Bill knot string the

   _____

3. brought party each something the child for

   _____

4. children street on the play kickball my

   _____

5. student new this is year Joanne a

   _____

6. favorite red my roses are flowers bright

   _____

7. new dentist gave toothbrush the me a

   _____

8. was with steak mushrooms our served brown

   _____

9. my took cleaners the I coat to

   _____

10. ticket name the it had lucky Sierra's on

   _____

Fragment or Sentence?

A **sentence fragment** is only a part of a sentence. It does not tell a complete thought.

fragment: After tomorrow, if I pass the test

sentence: After tomorrow, if I pass the test, I will graduate.

Write an **S** before each sentence that is complete. Write an **F** before each sentence fragment. Cross out the period on each fragment.

_____ 1. The pincushion cactus looks just like Mom's pincushion for sewing.

_____ 2. Prickly pear cactus and hedgehog cactus.

_____ 3. Sucks up water when it rains.

_____ 4. Spines help.

_____ 5. The agave and ocotillo thrive in the desert.

These are sentence fragments. Make each fragment a sentence by drawing a line to another fragment that completes the thought.

6. All cactuses	do not need a lot of water to live
7. Cactuses	can be white, yellow, red, or orange
8. Cactus flowers	can't eat cactuses with spines
9. Animals	stores water for dry spells.
10. The stem of the cactus	have roots close to the top of the ground.

Run-On Sentences

A **run-on sentence** has two or more complete thoughts that are not separated by punctuation. A run-on sentence needs to be divided.

run-on: I am a desert creature I love the heat I think I'll sit on this cactus all day.

correct: I am a desert creature, and I love the heat. I think I'll sit on this cactus all day.

Fix the run-on sentences in each description. Write the new sentences. Try to guess what each animal is.

I am a nocturnal animal and I shed my skin and I eat rodents, lizards, and even birds. I can inject my poison through my fangs and I have a rattle at the tip of my tail it tells when I may attack.

_____

_____

_____

_____

I am cold-blooded my body temperature is the same as the air around me and I am a tiny animal that looks like the giant dinosaurs that lived a long time ago.

_____

_____

_____

_____

Sentences: Subjects and Predicates

Every sentence has two parts. The **subject** tells who or what did something. The **predicate** tells what the subject does or did, or what the subject is or has.

Rachel	has a new bike.
who	**has**
The Drama Club	meets every Wednesday.
what	**does**

Underline the subject once and the predicate twice.

1. The horses are racing to the finish line.

2. Mrs. Pappas went to see Jack's teacher.

3. Josh moved to Atlanta, Georgia.

4. Monica's birthday is July 15.

5. The ball rolled into the street.

6. The policeman stopped the traffic.

7. Tisha planned a surprise party.

8. The winning team received a trophy.

9. The fireworks displays were fantastic.

10. The heavy rain drove everyone inside.

11. Adam looked everywhere for his book.

12. Can you hear the band outside?

13. Ben and Andre have just moved here.

14. The whole team is going to the soccer tournament.

15. My family has tickets for the football game.

Sentences: Subjects and Predicates

Underline the subject once and the predicate twice.

1. The telephone call was for me.

2. Mother baked a pumpkin pie.

3. Alicia fed the baby animals.

4. The American Indians passed the peace pipe.

5. The garden needs water to grow.

6. Lisa has beautiful long hair.

7. Dion and Ben played tennis.

8. Our family went apple picking.

9. The washing machine was broken.

10. My grandparents called me on my birthday.

11. Alex bought a new computer game.

12. We went on a float trip last summer.

13. My sister is getting a new car.

14. Brooke caught the ball on the first try.

15. Miguel tried to be first in line.

16. Khalil earned money for a new bike.

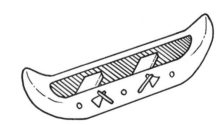

Sentences, Subjects, and Predicates: Review

Write a complete sentence using each subject.

1. The bears _____ .

2. The tunnel _____ .

3. Spencer _____ .

4. My camera _____ .

5. Snoopy _____ .

6. Danny and Amira _____ .

7. Thanksgiving _____ .

Write a complete sentence using each predicate.

8. _____ made me laugh.

9. _____ is 10 miles away.

10. _____ plays the piano.

11. _____ grows very well.

12. _____ woke up the campers.

13. _____ was brand new.

14. _____ are bright red.

Sentences, Subjects, and Predicates: Review

Write a complete sentence using each subject.

1. The truck _____ .

2. Mr. and Mrs. Taylor _____ .

3. The clowns _____ .

4. Fresh strawberries _____ .

5. Our team _____ .

6. A large crowd _____ .

7. Pancakes _____ .

8. All of the joggers _____ .

9. The skeleton _____ .

Write a complete sentence using each predicate.

10. _____ was funny.

11. _____ will be ready.

12. _____ went too quickly.

13. _____ is on the corner.

14. _____ were ruined.

15. _____ still exists.

16. _____ was fun.

17. _____ were on my desk.

18. _____ turned to gold.

Joining Sentences

When two or more **simple sentences** are joined together, they become a **compound sentence**. The conjunctions that may be used to join sentences are **and**, **but**, and **or**. Remember to place commas before these conjunctions.

Mayor Diaz hired a circus.
The circus came to town with clowns and animals.

Mayor Diaz hired a circus, **and** they came to town with clowns and animals.

Combine each pair of sentences using a comma and a conjunction. Write the new sentences.

1. Lanky Luke is as tall as the elephants. Delightful Denise is as short as her miniature pony.

   _____

   _____

2. Princess Penny always wears a party hat. Prince Pedro wears a beanie.

   _____

   _____

3. Fire Hydrant Felipe rides a tiny fire engine. His dalmatian rides with him.

   _____

   _____

4. Jingles likes to blow a tin horn. She likes to throw confetti.

   _____

   _____

Sentences: Statement or Question

Each kind of sentence does a different job. A **statement** is a sentence that tells something. It ends with a period.

I study French**.**

A **question** is a sentence that asks something. It ends with a question mark.

Do you study French**?**

Decide if each sentence is a **statement** or a **question**. Write the answer on the line. Place the correct ending mark at the end of each sentence.

1. Did you finish your homework   _____

2. Our grass needs cutting   _____

3. Our company is coming soon   _____

4. Sarah wore a heavy sweater   _____

5. Is that your lunchbox   _____

6. May I have some popcorn   _____

7. The music was too loud   _____

8. When is your birthday   _____

9. Have you seen Erik   _____

10. I need a map to get home   _____

11. Where is your notebook   _____

12. I need $1.00 for lunch   _____

Name_____

Sentences: Statement or Question

In each picture are two children. Give each child a name. Write a question one child might be asking the other. Place a question mark after each question.

Write the answer of the second child. Place a period after the answer.

1. Names: _____ and _____

    Question: _____

    Answer: _____

2. Names: _____ and _____

    Question: _____

    Answer: _____

3. Names: _____ and _____

    Question: _____

    Answer: _____

4. Names: _____ and _____

    Question: _____

    Answer: _____

Sentences: Exclamation or Command

A **command** is a sentence that tells someone to do something. A command ends with a period.

Stop talking**.**

An **exclamation** is a sentence that shows strong feelings, such as anger or excitement. It ends with an exclamation point.

This is so wonderful**!**

Decide if each sentence is a **command** or an **exclamation**. Write the answer on the line. Place the correct ending mark at the end of each sentence.

1.   Jill, feed the dog   _____

2.   I hate peas   _____

3.   Don't be late for your lesson   _____

4.   Answer the door   _____

5.   This water is too hot   _____

6.   Tony, make your bed   _____

7.   It's freezing in here   _____

8.   Get up at 7:00 am tomorrow   _____

9.   Your grades are marvelous   _____

10. Hang up your clothes   _____

11. This surprise party is great   _____

12. Those elephants are enormous   _____

Sentences: Ending Punctuation

A **period** is used
- at the end of statements and commands.   (We went home.)
- after an initial in a name.   (F. D. Roosevelt)
- after many abbreviations.   (Dr. Ave. in. Co.)

A **question mark** is used
- at the end of a question.   (Did you mail my letter?)

An **exclamation point** is used
- after an exclamation that shows strong feelings.   (Come quickly!)

Place periods, question marks, and exclamation points where they are needed.

1.   Thurs , Sept 7, is my birthday

2.   My neighbor works at J C Penney Inc

3.   Can you run one mile in 15 minutes

4.   Will you take a train to St Louis

5.   Eat your dinner

6.   The room measured 25 ft 4 in in length

7.   Did Chandra move to Price Dr last July

8.   Main St and 5th Ave is where Sara lives

9.   Hurry up and finish that right now

10.   Rev and Mrs R W Gonzalez live next door

11.   I bought a dozen apples for Ms Ormand

12.   My appointment with Dr Lee is at 2:30 pm

13.   The baby was born at 6 am and weighed 9 lb 13 oz

Sentences: Ending Punctuation

Read the paragraphs about the Grand Canyon. Add ending punctuation to separate the sentences and make their meaning clear.

The Grand Canyon has many trails These trails were made by deer, sheep, and the native people of the region When the sun sets, the canyon changes color How many colors can you see   It is very scary to look over the edge   The view is beautiful

On the canyon wall, we saw some Native American paintings The designs on the rocks are called pictographs They are symbols of objects from long ago Have you ever seen a pictograph

We saw people running the river Do you know what running the river is Climb aboard It's a chance to ride the Colorado River on a raft Wow You'll get the ride of your life

On another sheet of paper, write a paragraph about a trip you took to a special place. Use all four kinds of sentences: **statement, question, command,** and **exclamation**. Place the correct punctuation mark after each sentence.

Nouns

A **noun** is a word that names a  person, or place,  or thing.

Fill in each blank with the noun pictured.

1. My _____ was barking.

2. I like _____ to eat.

3. _____ is extremely cold.

4. A _____ has many colors.

5. The red _____ is pretty.

6. The living room _____ is on.

7. John rode the _____ to school.

8. Tia read her favorite _____ .

9. She had a _____ on her face.

10. I sat in a comfortable _____ .

11. I play the _____ well.

12. The _____ captured the stray dog.

13. Ben played outside in the _____ .

Proper Nouns

A **proper noun** is a noun that names a particular person, place, or thing. Proper nouns begin with capital letters.

Dr. John Shaw   Mulberry Street   Mount Everest

Write the proper nouns from each sentence on the scoreboard. Begin each proper noun with a capital letter.

1. My friend carla is from houston, texas.

2. I sent a letter to uncle chang.

3. I watched *mister ed* on television.

4. The lincoln memorial is in washington, d. c.

5. My aunt maria took me to see *star wars*.

6. In 1492, columbus discovered america.

7. Our first president was george washington.

8. I live on fifth street in new york.

9. I saw dr. tony silva when I was sick.

10. We camped in yellowstone national park.

○ ○ ○ ○ ○ SCOREBOARD ○ ○ ○ ○ ○				
1.	2.	3.	4.	5.
6.	7.	8.	9.	10.

Common Nouns and Proper Nouns

A **common noun** names a person, place, or thing.
A common noun begins with a lowercase letter.

dog   book

A **proper noun** names a particular person, place, or thing.
A proper noun begins with a capital letter.

Lassie   Sleeping Beauty

Write each noun in a bubble on the correct side. Begin each proper noun with a capital letter.

Proper Nouns   **Common Nouns**

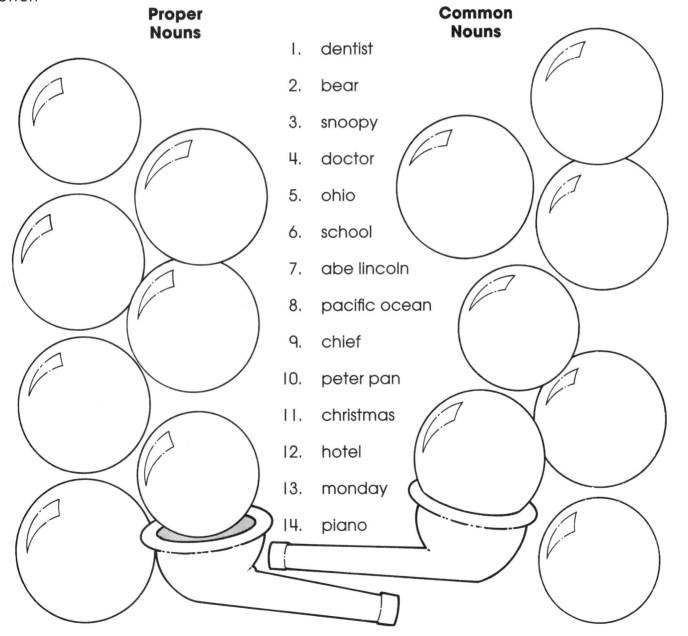

1. dentist
2. bear
3. snoopy
4. doctor
5. ohio
6. school
7. abe lincoln
8. pacific ocean
9. chief
10. peter pan
11. christmas
12. hotel
13. monday
14. piano

Common Nouns and Proper Nouns: Review

Look at each noun. If it is a **common noun,** copy it in the cloud titled *Common Nouns.* If it is a **proper noun,** change its first letter to a capital letter and copy it in the cloud titled *Proper Nouns.*

1. rhode island
2. dr. ross
3. ocean
4. thomas jefferson
5. dog
6. jan
7. new york
8. ice cream
9. mount everest

10. columbus
11. teacher
12. second avenue
13. park
14. sheriff

Common Nouns

Proper Nouns

Singular and Plural Nouns

A **singular noun** names one person, place, or thing.

The **class** went on a **field trip** to the **forest**.

A **plural noun** names more than one person, place, or thing.

The **classes** went on **field trips** to the **forests**.

Underline the singular nouns once and the plural nouns twice.

1. One girl saw three deer run across the field.

2. Squirrels were running up and down the sides of the trees.

3. A bunny scurried under a bush.

4. As the children watched, some Canadian geese flew overhead.

5. Pictures in books helped the children to identify many animals.

Write a sentence using each singular or plural noun.

6. (berries) _____

7. (city) _____

8. (trees) _____

9. (men) _____

10. (women) _____

11. (wrens) _____

12. (TV) _____

Plural Nouns

A **singular noun** names one person, place, or thing.

apple

A **plural noun** names more than one person, place, or thing. Usually, plural nouns end with an **s**.

apples

When a singular noun ends with **s**, **sh**, **ch**, or **x**, add **-es** to make it plural.

s—	loss**es**	bus**es**
sh—	brush**es**	bush**es**
ch—	peach**es**	bunch**es**
x—	box**es**	fox**es**

Write the plural of each noun.

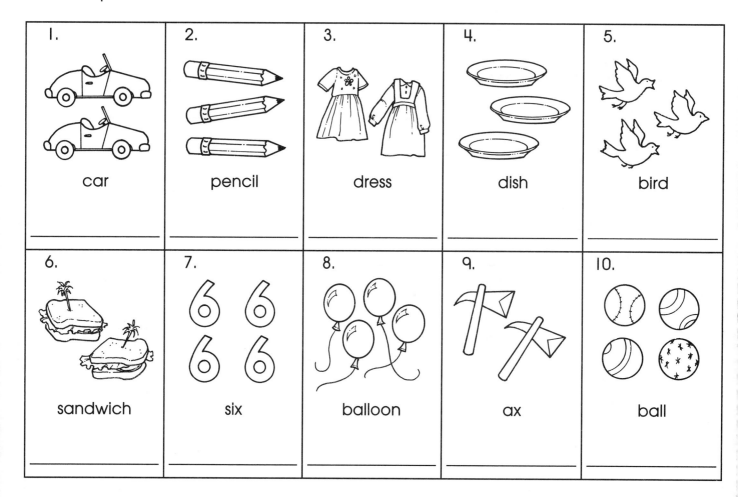

1. car

2. pencil

3. dress

4. dish

5. bird

6. sandwich

7. six

8. balloon

9. ax

10. ball

Plural Nouns

To form the plural of most nouns, add **-s**.

bananas    chairs

When s singular noun ends with **s**, **sh**, **ch**, or **x**, add **-es**.

boxes 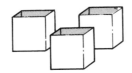   peaches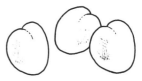

Write the plural of each noun.

1. bunch	2. class	3. wax
4. fox	5. brush	6. watch
7. bus	8. fix	9. light
10. wish	11. pass	12. switch
13. dish	14. church	15. report
16. trick	17. patch	18. ticket

1. _____	2. _____	3. _____
4. _____	5. _____	6. _____
7. _____	8. _____	9. _____
10. _____	11. _____	12. _____
13. _____	14. _____	15. _____
16. _____	17. _____	18. _____

Plural Nouns

When a singular noun ends in a consonant and **y**, change the **y** to **i** and add **-es**.

penny-pennies   fly-flies

Some singular nouns form their plural in special ways. There is no rule for these, so you have to memorize them.

man men   woman women   child children

foot feet   tooth teeth   mouse mice

Write the plural of each noun.

1. bunny   2. mouse   3. man

4. pony   5. tooth   6. boy

7. foot   8. child   9. cherry

10. party   11. candy   12. woman

1. _____   2. _____

3. _____   4. _____

5. _____   6. _____

7. _____   8. _____

9. _____   10. _____

11. _____   12. _____

Plural Nouns

When a singular noun ends in a consonant and **y**, change the **y** to **i** and add **-es**.

daisy   butterfly

daisies   butterflies

To some nouns ending in **f**, simply add **s**.

chief–chiefs   bluff–bluffs

To other nouns ending in **f** or **fe**, change the **f** or **fe** to **v** and add **-es**. There is no rule for these, so you have to memorize them.

calf calves   knife knives   loaf loaves   life lives

wolf wolves   shelf shelves   half halves   leaf leaves

Write the plural of each noun.

1. dwarf   2. calf   3. sky

4. cherry   5. cuff   6. leaf

7. knife   8. lady   9. army

10. roof   11. wolf   12. fairy

13. life   14. half   15. shelf

16. baby   17. belief   18. loaf

1. _____	2. _____	3. _____
4. _____	5. _____	6. _____
7. _____	8. _____	9. _____
10. _____	11. _____	12. _____
13. _____	14. _____	15. _____
16. _____	17. _____	18. _____

Plural Nouns

Some nouns are the same for both singular and plural. You must memorize them.

deer	salmon	trout	sheep	moose
tuna	cod	pike	bass	elk

Some singular nouns form their plurals in special ways. You must memorize them.

goose geese	person people	cactus cacti	tooth teeth
ox oxen	louse lice	die dice	mouse mice

Write the plural of each noun.

1. cod	2. trout	3. tuna
4. goose	5. elk	6. man
7. salmon	8. ox	9. child
10. woman	11. deer	12. bass
13. moose	14. foot	15. mouse
16. tooth	17. pike	18. sheep

1. _____	2. _____	3. _____
4. _____	5. _____	6. _____
7. _____	8. _____	9. _____
10. _____	11. _____	12. _____
13. _____	14. _____	15. _____
16. _____	17. _____	18. _____

Name_____

Plural Nouns: Review

Follow the path. Write the plural of each noun.

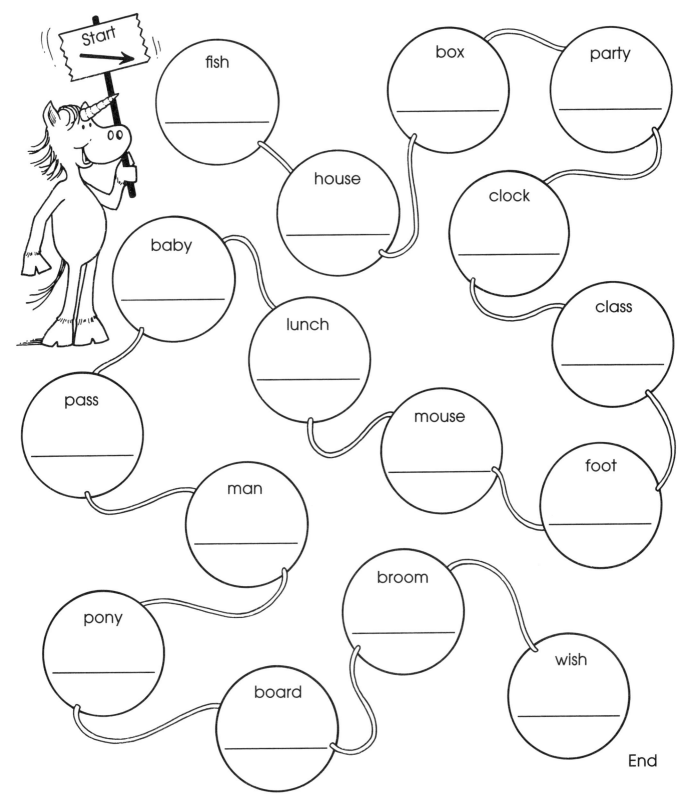

Start →

fish _____

box _____

party _____

house _____

clock _____

baby _____

lunch _____

class _____

pass _____

mouse _____

foot _____

man _____

broom _____

pony _____

wish _____

board _____

End

Name_____

Plural Nouns: Review

Write the plural of each noun.

wish _____	hobby _____	sheep _____	day _____
deer _____	bluff _____	child _____	boss _____
rash _____	cookie _____	match _____	knife _____
car _____	success _____	pony _____	foot _____
kiss _____	city _____	couch _____	mouse _____
woman _____	half _____	mirror _____	trout _____
person _____	tooth _____	dress _____	girl _____

Name_____

Possessive Nouns

A **possessive noun** shows ownership or possession. To make a singular noun show possession, add an apostrophe and **s**.

child**'s** toy   teacher**'s** book

Write a possessive noun for each phrase.

1.   the _____ bone

2.   the _____ nest

3.   the _____ cage

4.   the _____ petal

5.   the _____ nose

To make a plural noun that ends in **s** show possession, add an apostrophe after the **s**.

dogs**'** bones

To make a plural noun that does not end in **s** show possession, add an apostrophe and **s**.

children**'s** games

Write a possessive noun for each phrase.

6.   the _____ tails

7.   the _____ legs

8.   the _____ hoses

9.   the _____ whiskers

10. the _____ pages

Possessive Nouns

A **possessive noun** is a noun that shows possession.

To make a singular noun show possession, add an apostrophe and **s**.

       farmer**'s** rake   garden**'s** flower

If a plural noun ends in **s**, simply add an apostrophe.

       farmers**'** rakes    gardens**'** flowers

If a plural noun does not end in **s**, add an apostrophe and **s**.

       men**'s** shoes    women**'s** shoes

Write each group of words to make the noun show possession.

1. the toys of the children _____

2. the tail of the monkey _____

3. the cages of the animals _____

4. the balls of the bowlers _____

5. the house of my friend _____

6. the uniforms of the players _____

7. the backpack of Jill _____

8. the shoes of the runners _____

9. the paintings of the artist _____

10. the monitor of the computer _____

11. the hats of the men _____

12. the wife of my boss _____

Possessive Nouns

dog's bones   dogs' bones

Write the underlined noun to show possession by adding an apostrophe or apostrophe and **s**.

1. Mother took me to <u>Tony</u> house.   _____

2. The <u>chickens</u> eggs were large.   _____

3. <u>Jonathan</u> bicycle needs new brakes.   _____

4. Follow the <u>team</u> rules.   _____

5. The <u>shoes</u> soles need repair.   _____

6. Mrs. <u>Chu</u> car was in the driveway.   _____

7. My <u>brother</u> story won first prize.   _____

8. Our <u>neighbors</u> lawns need cutting.   _____

9. <u>Ellen</u> paintings were on display.   _____

10. The truck <u>drivers</u> routes were long.   _____

11. The <u>babies</u> toys are put away.   _____

12. The <u>principal</u> office is small.   _____

13. The <u>bird</u> nest is completed.   _____

14. The <u>doctors</u> hours were long.   _____

15. The <u>painter</u> brushes were clean.   _____

Possessive Nouns: Review

Write the underlined noun to show possession by adding an apostrophe or apostrophe and **s**.

1. The three <u>cats</u> paws were wet. _____

2. <u>Malia</u> pencil was broken. _____

3. Both <u>boys</u> grades were good. _____

4. This house is <u>Carson</u> house. _____

5. <u>Avery</u> aunt came to visit. _____

6. Some <u>flowers</u> leaves were large. _____

7. We saw two <u>bears</u> tracks. _____

8. The <u>children</u> room was messy. _____

9. My <u>sister</u> birthday is today. _____

10. The <u>clowns</u> acts made us laugh. _____

11. Noah filled <u>Rover</u> dish. _____

12. <u>Miguel</u> boys joined the game. _____

13. The baseball <u>players</u> uniforms are clean. _____

14. The <u>dog</u> dish was empty. _____

15. The <u>balloon</u> string is long. _____

Verbs

Verbs are words that show action or say that something is.
We **sailed** on Lake Michigan.   I **am** 10 years old.

Underline each verb.

1. Dad washed his new car in the driveway.

2. Nina took pictures with her new camera.

3. We numbered our paper from 1 to 10.

4. My friends need help with their homework.

5. Mother answered the doorbell in her apron.

6. I lost my new sweater at the game.

7. The students did their math on the board.

8. We painted our house white and green.

9. Sean ran the 100-yard dash at the track meet.

10. The whole class laughed at my jokes.

11. The chef baked delicious pies and cakes.

12. Jill slipped on the ice and broke her arm.

13. Khalil thought about his upcoming vacation.

14. Read the second chapter by tomorrow.

15. We looked through the microscope.

16. The boys ran and jumped over the fence.

17. The squirrels looked at us and then ran away.

18. Math is the subject most difficult for me.

19. My twin sisters are in the seventh grade.

20. My family was in Colorado when our car quit!

$$\begin{array}{r} 4 \\ \times\,3 \\ \hline 12 \end{array}$$

$$12-6=6$$

$$\begin{array}{r} 172 \\ +\,18 \\ \hline 190 \end{array}$$

Actions Verbs

Action verbs tell what a person or thing does.

Birds **fly**.   Dogs **run**.

Some action verbs tell about actions you can see. Others tell about actions you cannot see.

I **enjoyed** the game.   We **liked** the show.

Circle each action verb. Write it on a line.

1. raced	2. threw	3. sped	4. roared
5. traveled	6. went	7. popcorn	8. tiny
9. moon	10. player	11. adored	12. swam
13. viewed	14. divided	15. door	16. way
17. car	18. sewed	19. ruler	20. cried
21. sang	22. tennis	23. driver	24. worked
25. go	26. people	27. paints	28. eraser

_____   _____   _____   _____

_____   _____   _____   _____

_____   _____   _____   _____

_____   _____   _____   _____

Name_____

Action Verbs

Read the story about Macon's hike in the desert. Underline the action verb in each sentence.

The Unexpected Fall

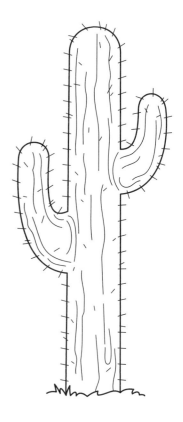

One Saturday, Macon and his father hiked in the desert near the Superstition Mountains. Macon ran ahead, anxious to see if he could find the Lost Dutchman's Gold Mine. Macon and his father looked up at the rocky mountain. Saguaro cactuses stood guard. White clouds scurried across the noon sky. The puffy white balls looked so close that Macon reached up to touch them.

As he jumped up, his father shouted, "Watch out!"

Macon saw the *Beware! Danger!* sign too late. Suddenly, his feet went out from under him, and he slid down a hole. When he stopped sliding, he was underground in the dark. He was in a cave. He heard his father yell, "Are you okay?"

Does Macon get out of the cave? Finish the story on another sheet of paper. Use action verbs.

Subject/Verb Agreement

The subject and verb in a sentence must agree in number.

An adult **plant makes** seeds.

Adult **plants make** seeds.

If the subject and verb agree, circle *Yes*. If they do not agree, circle *No*.

Yes   No   1. Seeds travel in many ways.

Yes   No   2. Sometimes, seeds falls in the water.

Yes   No   3. They may floats a long distance.

Yes   No   4. Animals gather seeds in the fall.

Yes   No   5. Squirrels digs holes to bury their seeds.

Yes   No   6. Cardinals likes to eat sunflower seeds.

Yes   No   7. The wind scatters seeds too.

Yes   No   8. Dogs carries seeds that are stuck in their fur.

Yes   No   9. Some seeds stick to people's clothing.

Yes   No   10. People plant seeds to grow baby plants called seedlings.

Subject/Verb Agreement

Subjects and verbs must agree in number. When the subject is one, it is singular. It should be matched to a singular verb. When the subject is more than one, it should be matched to a plural verb.

One of my friends **is** going to see the Grand Canyon.

There **are** 35 **students** on the bus.

Read about the student visitors in Arizona. Use the correct tense to make the subjects and verbs agree.

1. Last week, 35 students _____ on their way to the Grand Canyon.
   (to be)

2. One of the students _____ a fear of heights and _____ scared about
   (to have)   (to be)
   hiking down the narrow trails.

3. "There _____ one more stop before we get to the canyon," the bus driver said
   (to be)
   as he stopped the big bus.

4. When he stopped, there _____ 35 students who got off the bus and _____
   (to be)   (to go)
   to see the sands of the Painted Desert.

What did the boy who was afraid of heights do when the bus stopped at the "tall walls" of the Grand Canyon? Finish this story on another sheet of paper. Make sure your subjects and verbs agree.

Helping Verbs

A **helping verb** is used with an action verb. The most important verb is called the main verb and usually comes last. The other words in the verb are called helping verbs.

helping verbs	main verb
was	turning
should have	turned
must have been	turning

Study this wheel of helping verbs.

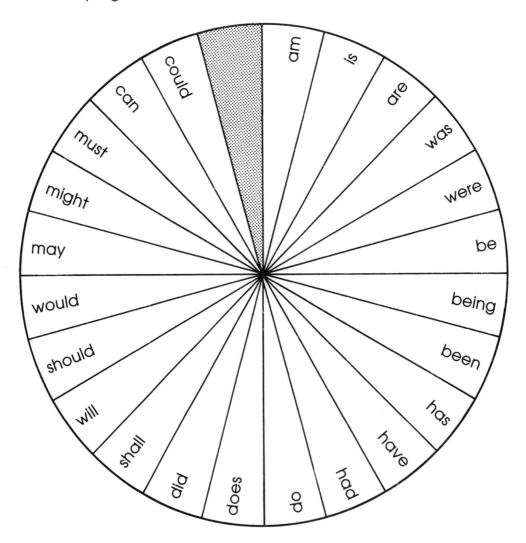

On another sheet of paper, write 10 sentences using helping verbs. Do not use any helping verb more than once.

Helping Verbs

A verb with more than one word has a **main verb** and one or more **helping verbs**.

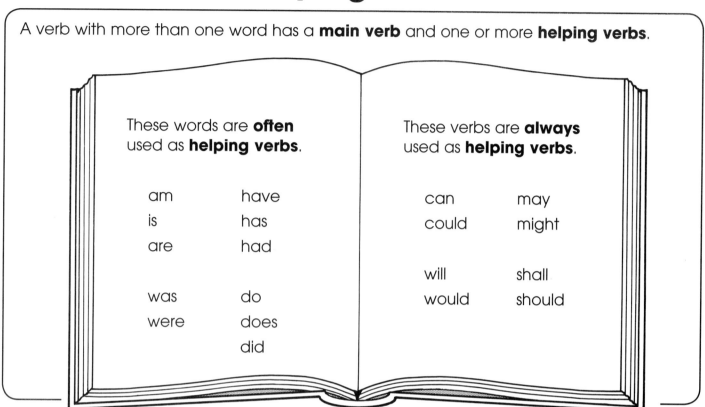

These words are **often** used as **helping verbs**.

am	have
is	has
are	had
was	do
were	does
	did

These verbs are **always** used as **helping verbs**.

can	may
could	might
will	shall
would	should

Underline the main verb once and the helping verbs twice.

1. Maria might spend the night.

2. The flowers are growing tall.

3. Matt is playing the piano for the play.

4. They were going to the movie.

5. Fernando should listen in class.

6. Liv should have eaten her vegetables.

7. I will be 12 on my next birthday.

8. I can do my homework later.

9. Vince has been working much too hard.

10. When are you going to finish the book?

Helping Verbs

Usually verbs that end in **-en** or **-ing** need helping verbs.

I **have written**. I **am writing**.

Underline the main verb once and the helping verbs twice.

1. We were going to the tennis match.

2. The children have eaten lunch already.

3. They must have been sleeping soundly.

4. We are going to the circus on Saturday.

5. Uncle Harry has driven to Houston.

6. You are playing the piano very well.

7. Benji was studying for the test.

8. The chocolate sauce will be adding the flavor to the dessert.

9. Jan is walking to the concert.

10. I am planning a party for my mother.

11. They have gotten a bib for the baby.

12. Wendy may be riding her bike to school.

13. Carlos and Gabe should be coming soon.

14. I have been cutting the grass.

Helping Verbs

Always use helping verbs with **been**, **seen**, **done**, and **gone**.

They **have been** ice skating.

Sometimes, helping verbs and main verbs are separated by words that are not verbs.

Mike **can** usually **win** in Scrabble.

Underline the main verb once and the helping verbs twice.

1. Have you seen my new car?

2. Carlos did not tell anyone his secret.

3. I am usually working on Saturday.

4. Dawn has gone to the meeting at school.

5. She is not going swimming in the lake.

6. You should never chew gum in class.

7. Felipe cannot get his locker open.

8. Did your older sister marry Trey?

9. I have been to my violin lesson.

10. I might not finish the large pizza.

11. Does the basketball game start at noon?

12. Quan can only play for one hour.

13. Was your mother angry about the window?

14. I am usually able to babysit on weekends.

15. I have never been to Hawaii, but I want to go!

16. Teaching school has always been my ambition.

17. Sara can often finish her homework before dinner.

18. Writing books is an enormous amount of work.

Verbs: Review

Underline the whole verb.

1. The music was loud in the room.

2. Leo has been watering the grass.

3. Pedro has gone to school for four years.

4. We stood for the national anthem.

5. Jill has eaten all of the popcorn.

6. Katie and Jessi are twins.

7. They have collected money for needy children.

8. Keisha will keep her cat inside.

9. Read the directions on the cover.

Circle the correct verb.

10. You (were, was) excellent in the talent show.

11. Maria and Erin (are, was) going to the zoo.

12. The policeman (is, are) directing traffic.

13. I (was, is) eating pizza.

14. Craig (be, has been) packing for his trip.

15. I (is, am) doing a puzzle for my project.

16. The birds (was, were) singing outside my window.

17. The children (are, is) looking forward to your visit.

Present Tense Verbs

Write the correct spelling for each verb to show present tense. Use the **-s** form.

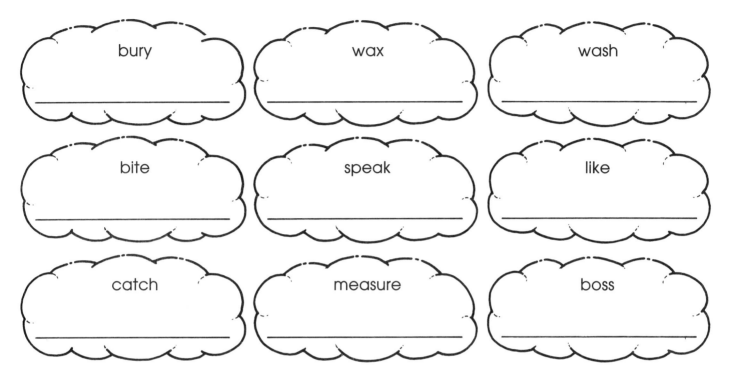

bury _____

wax _____

wash _____

bite _____

speak _____

like _____

catch _____

measure _____

boss _____

Circle the correct form of the verb.

1. My father (shave, shaves) every day.

2. The chorus (sing, sings) beautifully.

3. The ice cream cones (taste, tastes) delicious.

4. My neighbor (teach, teaches) French.

5. Megan (dash, dashes) to school every day.

6. The birds (fly, flies) from tree to tree.

7. Elm Street (cross, crosses) Main Street.

8. Michael and Kenyon (play, plays) tennis.

9. They (wait, waits) for the bus at the corner.

10. The clowns (make, makes) us laugh.

Past Tense Verbs

To make most verbs tell about the past, add **-ed** to the basic form.

walk walked   talk talked

Sometimes you must make spelling changes.

When the verb ends in a silent **e**, drop the **e** and add **-ed**.

rake raked   hope hoped

When the verb ends in **y** after a consonant, change the **y** to **i** and add **-ed**.

hurry hurried   try tried

When the verb ends in a single consonant after a single short vowel, double the final consonant and add **-ed**.

stop stopped   knit knitted

Write the past tense of each verb using the correct **-ed** ending.

1. study _____
2. bake _____
3. smell _____
4. wash _____
5. smile _____
6. grab _____
7. copy _____
8. trim _____

9. name _____
10. spy _____
11. melt _____
12. clip _____
13. toast _____
14. pop _____
15. empty _____
16. play _____

Past Tense Verbs

To make most verbs tell about the past, add **-ed** to the basic form.

cook cooked   clean cleaned

When the verb ends in a silent **e**, drop the **e** and add **-ed**.

rake raked   hope hoped

liked   typed

When the verb ends in **y** after a consonant, change the **y** to **i** and add **-ed**.

bury buried   spy spied

When the verb ends in a single consonant after a single short vowel, double the final consonant and add **-ed**.

drop dropped   trim trimmed

Write each verb using the correct **ed** ending.

dipped
begged

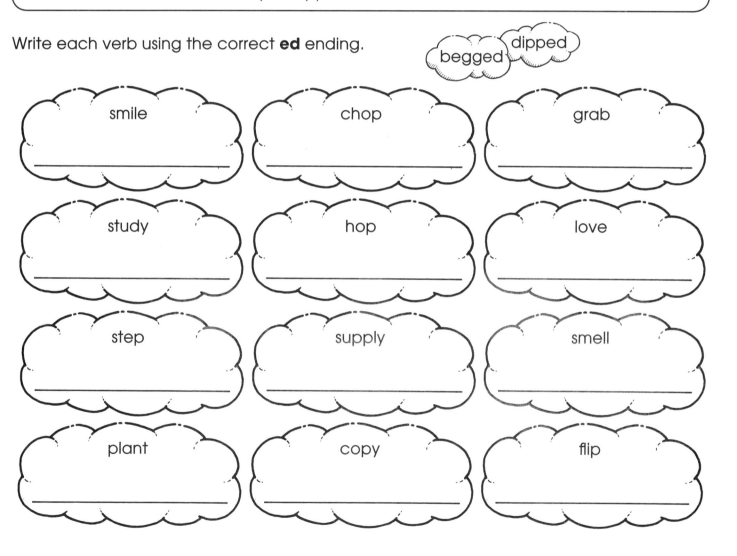

smile
_____

chop
_____

grab
_____

study
_____

hop
_____

love
_____

step
_____

supply
_____

smell
_____

plant
_____

copy
_____

flip
_____

Past Tense with Helping Verbs

Helping verbs can be used to tell about the past.

Use **has** with a singular subject.

   She has kicked the ball.

Use **have** with a plural subject or with *I* or *you*.

   The **boys have** kicked the ball.

Use **had** with a singular or plural subject.

   I had kicked the ball.   **They had** kicked the ball.

Write sentences with the verbs, a helping verb, and the correct **-ed** ending. Use only **has** or **have**.

1. stare   _____

2. bake   _____

3. worry   _____

4. jump   _____

5. arrive   _____

6. fix   _____

7. reply   _____

8. step   _____

9. change   _____

10. try   _____

11. brag   _____

12. close   _____

13. open   _____

14. ski   _____

Past Tense: Irregular Verbs

Irregular verbs change their basic form to show past tense.

eat ate   do did

Some of these verbs change their basic form again to show past tense with a helping verb.

eat ate has eaten   do did has done

Below are some irregular verbs you often use.

present	past	past with a helping verb
do	did	has done
eat	ate	has eaten
give	gave	has given
go	went	has gone
see	saw	has seen
take	took	has taken

Circle the correct form of the verb.

1. Danny (ate, eaten) a pizza for lunch.

2. The photographer (took, taken) my picture.

3. They (went, gone) to Disneyland.

4. We have (saw, seen) the Statue of Liberty.

5. Ginny was (gave, given) first prize.

6. My parents have (went, gone) to Detroit.

7. We (saw, seen) the greatest football game.

8. The class (took, taken) a field trip.

Past Tense: Irregular Verbs

To make a regular verb past tense, add **-d** or **-ed** to the verb. **Irregular verbs** do not form the past tense by adding **-d** or **-ed**.

regular verbs: paint painted   try tried

irregular verbs: fly flew   break broke

Rewrite the sentences in the past tense.

1. First, Aunt Becky picks out the paint for the shutters.

    _____

    _____

2. Then, Aunt Becky and Jenny shop for food for the picnic.

    _____

    _____

3. Next, they stop to get gas for the car.

    _____

    _____

4. After they shop, Aunt Becky asks Jenny to wash the car.

    _____

    _____

5. Finally, Aunt Becky's sisters arrive to have dinner.

    _____

    _____

Past Tense: Irregular Verbs

Verbs that show past tense in different ways are called **irregular verbs**. Below are seven commonly used irregular verbs.

present	past	past with helping verb
break	broke	has broken
bring	brought	has brought
come	came	has come
drive	drove	has driven
do	did	has done
eat	ate	has eaten
give	gave	has given

Circle the correct form of the verb.

1. We (ate, eaten) all the birthday cake.

2. Ella (came, come) to my piano recital.

3. Dad has (gave, given) me my allowance.

4. Mom (drove, driven) me to my soccer game.

5. Last night, I (did, done) my homework.

6. My sister has (came, come) home from college.

7. Our TV has been (broke, broken) for a week.

8. Jimmy has (drove, driven) to Los Angeles.

9. Craig had (ate, eaten) too much ice cream.

10. I (broke, broken) my arm skiing in Colorado.

11. Elizabeth (did, done) me a big favor.

12. We have (gave, given) the problem much thought.

13. The Jungs (gave, give) a donation to the Red Cross.

Past Tense: Irregular Verbs

Write the past tense of each irregular verb.

1. Sam almost _____ (fall) when he tripped over the curb.

2. Diandre made sure she _____ (take) bug spray on her hike.

3. Dave _____ (run) over to his friend's house.

4. Mario _____ (break) off a long piece of grass to put in his mouth.

5. Erica _____ (know) the path along the river well.

6. The clouds _____ (begin) to turn gray.

7. Kasey _____ (throw) a small piece of bread to the ducks.

8. Everyone _____ (eat) a very nutritious meal after the long adventure.

9. We all _____ (sleep) very well that night.

10. The moon _____ (shine) brightly in the night sky.

11. The morning _____ (bring) a brand new day.

12. Everyone _____ (begin) to arise from their beds.

Irregular Verbs

Below are seven frequently used irregular verbs.

present	past	past with helping verb
grow	grew	has grown
go	went	has gone
run	ran	has run
see	saw	has seen
take	took	has taken
throw	threw	has thrown
write	wrote	has written

Circle the correct form of the verb.

1. Our gym class (ran, run) the 50-yard dash.

2. My car should have (went, gone) to the repair shop.

3. Amira (saw, seen) the magic show.

4. Cody (threw, thrown) a snowball at Michael.

5. We have (ran, run) out of sugar.

6. Shannon has (wrote, written) a letter to Kate.

7. We (took, taken) many beautiful pictures of sunsets.

8. We have (saw, seen) the Super Bowl.

9. After it rained, my flowers (grew, grown).

10. We (went, gone) on a boat ride last July.

11. Have you (took, taken) out the trash?

12. I was (threw, thrown) from my horse.

13. Have you (threw, thrown) the dead plant away?

14. We had (went, gone) to the mall when it happened.

Past Tense Verbs: Review

Write the correct spelling for the past tense of each verb.

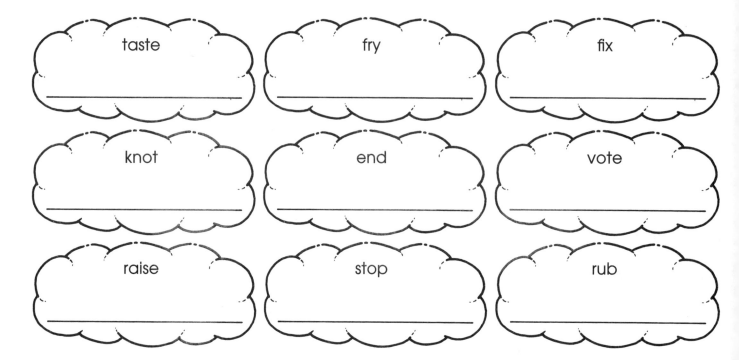

taste
_____

fry
_____

fix
_____

knot
_____

end
_____

vote
_____

raise
_____

stop
_____

rub
_____

Circle the correct form of the verb.

1. You have (ate, eaten) too many cookies.

2. Donna had (saw, seen) the ice show.

3. We (took, taken) flowers to Grandma.

4. Our family (went, gone) to the beach.

5. Josh should have (did, done) the dishes.

6. Have you been (gave, given) the assignment?

7. We (ate, eaten) popcorn at the movie.

8. Mother had (took, taken) Jeff to the dentist.

9. After it rained, we (saw, seen) a rainbow.

10. Dad had (went, gone) on a business trip.

Future Tense Verbs

Verbs in the **future tense** usually add the verb **will** to tell what will happen.

He **will** work.

Chang and Torrance are going on safari in the jungle. They wrote a journal entry about what they thought they would see on their adventure. Circle all of the verbs that are in the future tense.

In the Jungle

We will walk through the hot, dark jungle. Who will go with us on our jungle

adventure? Will you make a face like a monkey or squawk like a parrot? Tigers will growl

and roar. We will eat our lunch under a giant fern. After lunch, we will pick papaya,

bananas, and mangoes. I hope a hungry gorilla will join us for lunch. What will a gorilla

look like wearing your hat? We will share our bananas.

Write a paragraph about a trip you would like to take. Use verbs in the future tense.

_____

_____

_____

_____

_____

_____

_____

Future Tense Verbs

Underline the verb in each sentence. Then, change the verb to show future tense. Write the new verb on the line after each sentence.

1. Where in the world are the pyramids? _____

2. We look for the answer in the encyclopedia or world atlas. _____

3. We find pyramids in Central and South America and Egypt. _____

4. The explorers visit the pyramid of Cheops in Egypt. _____

5. The explorers study the history of the pyramids and their architecture.
   _____

6. The team compares the pyramids in Egypt with the pyramids in Central and South America. _____

7. After they finish visiting the pyramids, the explorers write a book about what they saw. _____

8. One of the team members, the photographer, donates his pictures to the project. _____

9. A university press publishes 10,000 copies of their book. _____

10. The group receives royalties on the sales of the book for 10 years.
    _____

Future Tense Verbs

Here is a list that Aunt Grace had on her refrigerator. Rewrite each sentence in the future tense.

1. This afternoon, I pick up groceries at the store.

   _____

   _____

2. I call the painter to paint the shutters.

   _____

   _____

3. The neighborhood builds a float for the parade next Friday.

   _____

   _____

4. The picnic lunch at City Hall is tomorrow.

   _____

   _____

5. Jenny comes on Thursday.

   _____

   _____

6. The violin quartet plays on Saturday.

   _____

   _____

Pronouns

helpful hints	singular	plural
Pronouns are words that take the place of singular or plural nouns.		
pronouns used to talk about yourself	I, me	we, us
pronouns used to talk to the person	you	you
pronouns used to talk about other persons or things	he, him, it, she, her	they, them

Write the pronoun in the party favor.

1. Nadia had her teeth cleaned.

2. Is Mother going with us?

3. Do you like chocolate pie?

4. Tony is taking him a present.

5. They watched the football game.

6. Dad gave them some money.

7. I watched cartoons on TV.

8. We went fishing yesterday.

9. Kayla gave me an apple.

10. He bought a new game.

Pronouns

A **pronoun** is used in place of a noun.

If the pronoun is the subject, use **I**, **we**, **he**, or **she**.

Oliver plays the violin.	Mia plays the piano.
He plays the violin.	**She** plays the piano.

If the pronoun is not the subject, use **me**, **us**, **her**, **him**, or **them**. The pronoun is an object.

Mother took Chloe shopping.	Dad went fishing with Alex.
Mother took **her** shopping.	Dad went fishing with **him**.

Use **it** and **you** as a subject or an object.

The bicycle is new.	I waited for the bus.
It is new.	I waited for **it**.

Circle the correct pronoun and write it on the line.

1. Danny and (me, I) went camping. _____

2. (We, Us) went to the baseball game. _____

3. The teacher took (we, us) to the library. _____

4. (Him, He) was a famous American. _____

5. Aunt Mona gave $1.00 to (them, we). _____

6. (Her, You) and Greg are my best friends. _____

7. Please take this note to (he, him). _____

8. Chase took Adam and (me, I) to the party. _____

9. The teacher told (she, her) to talk louder. _____

10. You and (he, him) gave a good report. _____

Pronouns

A **pronoun** is a word that takes the place of a noun or nouns in a sentence. Some pronouns take the place of subjects. Some pronouns take the place of objects.

subject pronouns: I, you, he, she, it, we, they

object pronouns: me, you, him, her, it, us, them

Write the correct pronouns above each sentence to replace the underlined nouns.

1. As <u>the *Nautilus*</u> cruised along the shore, <u>the crew</u> could see <u>surfers</u> riding huge waves.

2. When <u>the submarine</u> docked, <u>hundreds of sailors</u> were on the wharf to greet the ship.

3. After <u>everyone</u> had left <u>the ship,</u> <u>the captain</u> received orders for another assignment.

4. <u>The message</u> asked that <u>the crew and the submarine</u> be ready to depart for Mexico.

5. <u>The captain</u> knew where <u>the *Nautilus*</u> was going next.

6. The trip had something to do with <u>whales</u>.

7. There are a lot of <u>whales</u> in the Gulf region because <u>the water</u> is warmer there.

Pronouns

Read the sentences. In the blank after each pronoun, write the word or words that the pronoun takes the place of.

Most penguins live near the South Pole. They _____ spend most of their time underwater searching for food. Penguins surface for air and get enough of it _____ to fill the air sacs throughout their bodies. These _____ make it possible for them _____ to stay underwater for long periods of time.

Although penguins have wings, they _____ are not used for flying. Their wings are like flippers. They _____ are used for swimming.

Penguins feel best in very cold water but leave it _____ to nest and raise their young. A penguin's nest is very odd. It _____ is simply a pile of stones on a rocky shore. The female lays from one to three eggs. They _____ are chalky white. After a time, the female passes her eggs on to the male. He _____ tucks them _____ into a skin flap under his body to keep them _____ warm. It _____ is lined with thick, soft down. The parents take turns feeding the babies when they _____ hatch.

At first, the babies are covered with down. Later, they _____ grow feathers on their bodies and scaly feathers on their wings. Before long, they _____ go to sea with the adults to catch fish.

Possessive Pronouns

Pronouns that show ownership are called **possessive pronouns**. Some are used with nouns.

his dog   **her** cat   **our** pets

Some possessive pronouns are used without nouns.

The dog is **mine**.   The cat is **hers**.

pronouns used with a noun			pronouns used without a noun		
my	his	their	mine	his	theirs
our	her		ours	hers	
your	its		yours	its	

Write a new sentence using a possessive pronoun in place of the underlined words.

1. This house is <u>Clay's house</u>.

   _____

2. <u>Nicole's</u> friends came for dinner.

   _____

3. <u>Abbie and Jessi's</u> school is large.

   _____

4. That bicycle is <u>my bicycle</u>.

   _____

5. This game is <u>your game</u>.

   _____

6. Pancake is <u>Bill's dog</u>.

   _____

Possessive Pronouns

The possessive form of a pronoun does not use an apostrophe. These are the possessive forms of pronouns.

my, mine	our, ours
your, yours	you, yours
his, her, hers, its	their, theirs
The dog lost **her** tag.	The twins rode **their** bikes.

Write the correct possessive pronoun on the line using the information in the parentheses.

1. Comb _____ hair.
   (The hair belongs to you.)

2. The baby boy took _____ bottle.
   (The bottle belongs to the baby.)

3. The books were _____ .
   (The books belonged to Jimmy.)

4. The _____ color was red.
   (The color belonged to the ball.)

5. The mailman brought _____ mail.
   (The mail belonged to us.)

6. _____ flowers are in bloom.
   (The flowers belong to me.)

7. The blue bicycle is _____ .
   (The bicycle belongs to you.)

8. _____ piano lesson is today.
   (The piano lesson is Jill's.)

9. _____ TV is broken.
   (The TV belongs to us.)

Pronouns: Review

Read the story about Renee's dream. Underline each pronoun.

A Scary Dream

"They are coming after us," Renee said to her brother, Scott. "Believe me, Scott, I saw them with their funny-looking faces. The two of them had long orange hair, and they had gigantic feet. I thought they could be from Mars because they spoke a funny language.

One of them glared at me with his strange-looking face. The other one looked like she had on her clothes from outer space.

Scott, you can't imagine my thoughts as I saw them coming after me with their weird looks and their weird clothes."

Finish this story. Use at least six different pronouns. Circle the pronouns you use.

_____

_____

_____

_____

_____

_____

_____

_____

Adjectives

An **adjective** is a word that describes a noun.

adjectives	tell what kind	**bright** sun
	tell how many	**two** birds
	tell which ones	**this** tree

Complete each sentence with an adjective that describes each picture.

This shelf had _____ books.

This is a _____ bus.

_____ bike is mine.

This is a _____ rose.

Look at the _____ kites.

This person is a _____ person.

This camel has _____ humps.

This looks like a _____ hamburger.

This tree has _____ leaves.

This _____ clown was at the party.

This car has a _____ dent.

This dog has a _____ nose.

Adjectives

An **adjective** is a word that describes a noun or pronoun.
Adjectives
- tell what kind.   (**kitchen** table, **card** table)
- tell how many.   (**seven** pencils, **many** pencils)
- tell which ones.   (**this**, **that**, **these**, **those**)

Write an adjective on each line. Do not use the same adjective more than once.

1. My _____ skirt is plaid.

2. My _____ friend has _____ eyes.

3. The _____ weather was good for our garden.

4. _____ hat keeps my head warm.

5. The campers put up _____ tents.

6. Ben went to a _____ movie.

7. Mother picked up our _____ toys and _____ clothes.

8. We made a _____ , _____ vase in art class.

9. Dad is a _____ tennis player.

10. I saw _____ bears and _____ bison at the park.

11. Holly used her _____ calculator.

12. Our _____ dog is a _____ pet.

13. That _____ building is very _____ .

14. Sarah just got a _____ car and a _____ dog.

15. The _____ , _____ music drove my mom crazy.

Adjectives

Write five adjectives that could describe the picture in the center of each flower. Do not use the same adjective more than once.

Adjectives

Write three adjectives that describe each noun. Do not use the same adjective more than once.

ball	feet	house
airplane	hot dog	cloud
butterflies	shoes	bells
manatee	flowers	ice-cream cone

Name_____

Adjectives

Write an adjective on each line. Do not use the same adjective more than once.

1. The _____ clouds in the _____ sky were

   _____ and _____ ones.

2. In the _____ morning, the _____

   children went to the _____ beach.

3. The _____ smell of the _____ pizza

   made the _____ children happy.

4. One _____ afternoon, my _____ friends

   and I went to a _____ cave in the

   _____ woods near my _____ house.

5. The _____ creatures on the _____

   planet looked like _____ , _____ men.

6. The _____ animals in the _____ park

   were _____ and _____ looking.

7. _____ children in our _____ class saw

   the _____ movie about the _____ people

   from the _____ place.

fluffy cloud

rain cloud

Adjectives

Add **-er** to an adjective when you compare two people, places, or things.

smaller child   louder noise

Add **-est** to an adjective when you compare three or more people, places, or things.

smallest child   loudest noise

Circle the correct form of the adjective in the parentheses.

1. Of the two towels, this one feels (softer, softest).

2. His story was the (longer, longest) one in his class.

3. Which of these two bananas is (smaller, smallest)?

4. The prices at Xia's store are the (lower, lowest) in town.

5. The kitchen is the (warmer, warmest) room in our house.

6. This cake is (sweeter, sweetest) than that pie.

7. Yesterday was the (colder, coldest) day we've had this winter.

8. Kenyon is the (taller, tallest) of the twins.

9. My desk is the (neater, neatest) of the two.

10. Roberto is the (faster, fastest) runner on the team.

11. Let's watch the (shorter, shortest) movie on TV.

12. Which one of your parents is (older, oldest)?

13. Samia chose the (smaller, smallest) of the two kittens.

14. The redwood is the (larger, largest) tree in the world.

Name_____

Adjectives

When an adjective ends in a single consonant after a single short vowel, double the final consonant and add **-er** or **-est**.

bigger   biggest

When an adjective ends in a silent **e**, drop the final **e** and add **-er** or **-est**.

wider   widest

If an adjective ends in **y** after a consonant, change the **y** to **i** and add **-er** or **-est**.

sillier   silliest

Write the two forms each adjective uses when comparing two things and three or more things.

		Two Things	Three or More Things
1.	easy	_____	_____
2.	brave	_____	_____
3.	scary	_____	_____
4.	red	_____	_____
5.	nice	_____	_____
6.	hungry	_____	_____
7.	blue	_____	_____
8.	noisy	_____	_____
9.	flat	_____	_____
10.	fast	_____	_____

Name_____

Adjectives

Longer adjectives are usually compared by using **more** and **most**.

Use **more** to compare two people, places, or things.

Dave is **more helpful** than Pete.

Use **most** to compare three or more people, places, or things.

Holly was the **most helpful** student in the class.

If you use *more* or *most*, do not use **-er** or **-est**.

right: This tree is **larger** than that one.

wrong: This tree is **more larger** than that one.

Circle the correct form of the adjective.

1. This is the (more useful, most useful) book in the library.

2. Brand X keeps my clothes (cleaner, more cleaner) than Brand Y.

3. The movie was the (most scariest, scariest) I've ever seen.

4. As an artist, Donna is the (more talented, most talented) of the twins.

5. Rick is (more taller, taller) than his dad.

6. Of all the flavors, chocolate is the (more delicious, most delicious).

7. Nikki's joke was (funnier, more funnier) than mine.

8. Ellen's report was the (most neatest, neatest) one in her class.

9. That rose is the (more unusual, most unusual) one I have.

10. Nathan picked the (more biggest, biggest) apple on the tree.

Adjectives

A few adjectives change to completely new words when they are used to compare things. Two of these adjectives are the words **good** and **bad**.

good—This is a **good** book.

better—My book is **better** than your book.

best—This is the **best** book I've ever read.

bad—The weather is **bad** today.

worse—The weather is **worse** today than yesterday.

worst—Today's weather is the **worst** of the winter.

Circle the correct form of the adjective.

1. This is the (bad, worse, worst) pizza I have ever eaten.

2. My shoes are in (bad, worse, worst) condition than yours.

3. My grades are the (good, better, best) in the class.

4. Mother has a (good, better, best) attitude about the flood.

5. This tool is the (good, better, best) one I have.

6. I wore my (bad, worse, worst) pair of jeans to the painting party.

7. My brownies taste (good, better, best) than yours.

8. This is a (bad, worse, worst) snowstorm.

9. This one looks even (good, better, best) than that one.

10. My brother's room looks (bad, worse, worst) than mine.

11. Your tennis shoes have the (good, better, best) soles.

12. This headache is the (bad, worse, worst) I've ever had.

good   better   best

Nouns and Adjectives: Review

Underline the adjectives and circle the nouns they describe. Do not underline **a** or **an**.

1. Dad bought a new, blue car.

2. This winter has been cold and icy.

3. The furry cat hid under my back porch.

4. The brave firefighter rescued the small children.

5. My parents bought a new table and lamp.

6. Many birds ate from our large birdfeeder.

7. The American flag is red, white and blue.

8. Jeff has one brother and two sisters.

9. I needed a sharp knife to cut the tough meat.

10. The handsome man married the beautiful woman.

11. The mysterious spaceship landed in the dense forest.

12. The chocolate cupcakes were on the large plate.

13. The longest race of the day lasted one hour.

14. Your tennis shoes look newer than mine.

15. The young children walked along the sandy beach.

16. Ten clowns climbed out of the tiny car.

17. The dog chased the little black kitten up a tree.

18. Sarah made six bibs for her tiny nephew.

19. Many people attended the big race last Saturday.

20. The funniest act had the two crazy clowns.

Prepositions

Prepositions are words that relate nouns to other words in a sentence. They show where a noun is going, how it might be going, or to whom it might be going. Some prepositions are **in**, **with**, **on**, **beneath**, and **about**.

I played computer games **with** my best friend.

Underline the prepositions.

1. The tree fell behind the house.

2. I saw the movie with Sara.

3. I stepped outside the circle.

4. Don't play golf in the rain.

5. I put my book next to the TV.

6. The painter climbed up the ladder.

7. We had recess inside today.

8. The driver raced around the corner.

9. The pot fell off the table.

10. The cat was hiding under the bed.

Prepositions

Prepositions relate one word in a sentence to another by location, direction, cause, or possession. A preposition, and its object and modifiers is called a **prepositional phrase**.

I walked **beside the road**.

Circle each preposition. Then, underline the rest of the phrase.

1. I boarded the train at the whistle's blow.

2. I sat down by a woman in a purple dress and hat.

3. Just as I sat down, the conductor asked for my ticket.

4. We had to go to the club car for lunch.

5. For lunch, we had tomato soup, potato salad, and ham sandwiches.

6. After lunch, the conductor said, "Two hours to Littleville."

7. "I think I'll take a short nap," said the woman in the purple dress.

8. My seat was by the window.

9. I spent the rest of the trip watching the world go by.

10. At three in the afternoon, we arrived in Littleville.

Adverbs

An **adverb** answers the questions how, when, or where about verbs. Many adverbs end in **-ly** when answering the question how.

Our team won the game <u>easily</u>. (How?)

Circle the adverb in each sentence. In the book, write which question it answers.

1. The children played quietly at home.

2. We went to the movie yesterday.

3. My friends are coming inside to play.

4. The child cut his meat carefully.

5. The girls went upstairs to get their coats.

6. The play-off games start tomorrow.

7. The boys walked slowly toward the bus.

8. The teacher said, "Write your name neatly."

9. We ate outside on a picnic table.

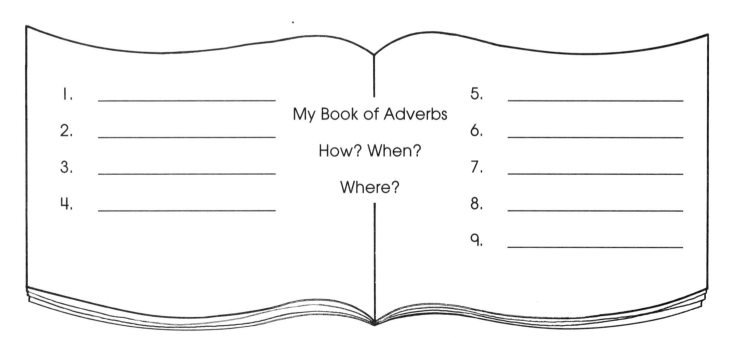

1. _____

2. _____

3. _____

4. _____

My Book of Adverbs

How? When?

Where?

5. _____

6. _____

7. _____

8. _____

9. _____

Adverbs

Adverbs modify verbs or adjectives and tell how, when, or where.

how—I read **slowly**.

where—I read **inside**.

when—I was reading **today**.

Write **how, when**, or **where** after each adverb.

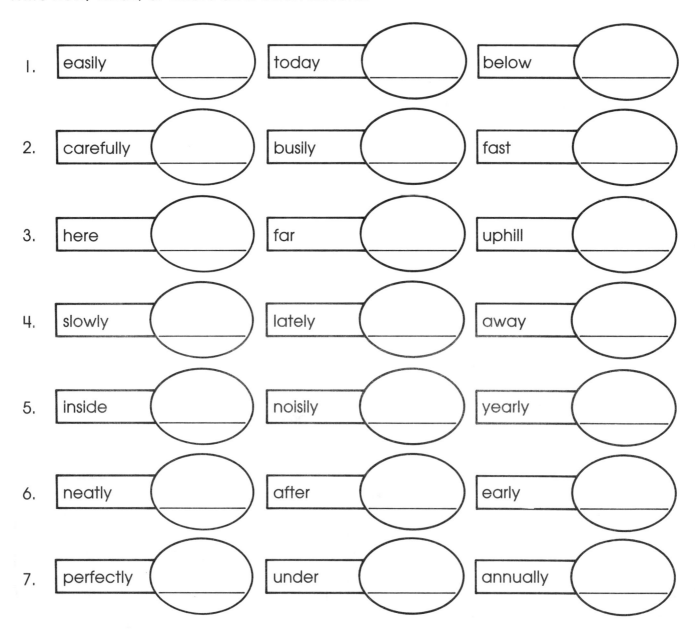

1. easily   today   below

2. carefully   busily   fast

3. here   far   uphill

4. slowly   lately   away

5. inside   noisily   yearly

6. neatly   after   early

7. perfectly   under   annually

Adverbs

Write an adverb to complete each sentence. The word in parentheses tells the kind of adverb to write. Do not use the same adverb more than once.

1. Our team played _____ . (when)

2. Brian writes _____ . (how)

3. The cows move _____ . (how)

4. Melissa will dance _____ . (when)

5. My dog went _____ . (where)

6. We ran _____ . (how)

7. The choir sang _____ . (how)

8. The cat purred _____ . (where)

9. Hannah spoke _____ . (how)

10. We'll go on our vacation _____ . (when)

11. The sign goes _____ . (where)

12. Mother brought the groceries _____ . (where)

13. David read the directions _____ . (how)

14. We'll be leaving _____ . (when)

15. We have three bedrooms _____ . (where)

16. Our family goes on a vacation _____ . (when)

17. Jim ran _____ down the street. (how)

18. They _____ laid the baby in the crib. (how)

19. The man went _____ with his paper. (where)

20. My dad gets a raise in pay _____ . (when)

Name_____

Adverbs

Sometimes, people have difficulty using *good, well, sure, surely, real,* and *really* correctly. This chart will help you use adjectives and adverbs correctly.

Adjectives	Adverbs
Good is an adjective when it describes a noun. That was a **good** dinner.	**Good** is never used as an adverb.

Well is an adjective when it means in good health or having a good appearance.
 	
    She looks **well**.
	Well is an adverb when it is used to tell that something is done capably or effectively.
	
	    She writes **well**.

Sure is an adjective when it modifies a noun.
 	
    A robin is a **sure** sign of spring.
	Surely is an adverb.
	
	    He **surely** wants a job.

Real is an adjective that means genuine or true.
 	
    That was a **real** diamond.
	Really is an adverb.
	
	    Maria **really** played a good game.

Write the correct word to finish the sentence. Use the chart to help you.

1.   You did a very _____ job cleaning your room. (good, well)

2.   The detective in the story used his skills _____ . (good, well)

3.   Lee _____ wanted to finish before everyone else. (sure, surely)

4.   I _____ want to read that book now. (real, really)

5.   Did it take you long to decide who the _____ criminal was? (real, really)

6.   The hamster looked _____ and healthy, but he got sick. (well, good)

7.   Kyle read _____ as he worked on the story problem. (well, good)

8.   You will _____ get a good grade on that report. (sure, surely)

Verbs and Adverbs: Review

Underline the adverbs and circle the verbs. Write each verb and adverb in the proper column.

	Verb	Adverb
1. Jason got his bicycle early.	_____	_____
2. Slowly, I cleaned my room.	_____	_____
3. Lucy often rides her horse.	_____	_____
4. We walked cautiously on the ice.	_____	_____
5. I washed my car today.	_____	_____
6. Suddenly, it started to snow.	_____	_____
7. Derek took his wagon outside.	_____	_____
8. The child used the scissors carefully.	_____	_____
9. Jackie went home early.	_____	_____
10. Bill slid safely into second base.	_____	_____
11. Sierra happily got 100% on her test.	_____	_____
12. My cousin came again to visit.	_____	_____
13. Earlier, I helped the principal.	_____	_____
14. The soldiers bravely fought.	_____	_____
15. We quickly finished the puzzle.	_____	_____
16. Yesterday, I baked brownies.	_____	_____
17. Renee takes her shower upstairs.	_____	_____
18. My dad gets his paycheck monthly.	_____	_____
19. The twins threw the toys everywhere.	_____	_____
20. The mouse crept out quietly.	_____	_____

Nouns, Pronouns, Adjectives, Verbs, and Adverbs: Review

Label each of the following above the words.

N—noun   **Adj**—adjective

P—pronoun   **Adv**—adverb

V—verb

1. We feed the birds regularly.

2. Derek planted a maple tree yesterday.

3. Chang wrote them a letter.

4. They have two small dogs.

5. Ruby will be dancing tomorrow.

6. The toys were everywhere.

7. The three children are going swimming today.

8. You can eat now.

9. They washed the car carefully.

10. Several thirsty children drank cold lemonade.

11. We run three miles often.

12. The chorus has been singing beautifully.

13. He gave Chris five dollars.

14. Paige washed the dishes slowly.

15. That tiny baby was sleeping soundly.

Articles

Use **a** before words beginning with consonants.

a bird   a blue bird

Use **an** before words beginning with vowels.

an apple   an orange

Only use **a** or **an** before singular nouns.

a cow   an animal

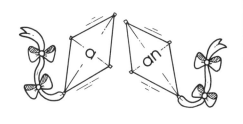

Write **a** or **an** on each line.

1. I have _____ aunt named Mary.

2. We went to _____ movie last night.

3. Mark wrote _____ long letter.

4. We took _____ English test.

5. Neil has _____ old bicycle.

6. We each had _____ ice cream cone.

7. Mandy ate _____ orange for breakfast.

8. They saw _____ deer on their trip.

9. Stephen thought the car was _____ ugly color.

10. Emily bought _____ new pair of skates.

11. He was _____ officer in the army.

12. We built _____ campfire.

13. _____ elephant is such a large animal.

14. The group went to _____ interesting museum.

Articles

Circle the correct word.

1. Mark has (a, an) orange and brown sweater.

2. Two quarters equal (a, an) half dollar.

3. (A, An) engine pulled (a, an) long train.

4. They put up (a, an) target in the field.

5. There is (a, an) enormous house on (a, an) hill.

6. My family went to (a, an) opera in New York.

7. We talked to (a, an) teacher about (a, an) answer.

8. Mia had (a, an) art lesson after school.

9. I got (a, an) infield hit in the big game!

10. (A, An) exit sign hung over (a, an) door.

11. We had (a, an) aunt and (a, an) uncle come for dinner.

12. We each had (a, an) cookie and (a, an) ice cream cone.

13. Vince ran for (a, an) hour on (a, an) cinder track.

14. Jimmy learned (a, an) Indian dance on (a, an) reservation.

15. (A, An) honest friend is someone to treasure.

Contractions

Contractions are made by putting together two words. When the words are combined, one or two letters are left out. An apostrophe is used in place of the missing letters.

word + will	I will → I'll
word + is	she is → she's
word + has	he has → he's
word + are	they are → they're
word + have	they have → they've
word + not	has not → hasn't
word + would	he would → he'd

Write a contraction for each pair of words.

1. is not	2. she is	3. they have	4. he is
5. I would	6. you are	7. she will	8. did not
9. he will	10. where is	11. they would	12. she has

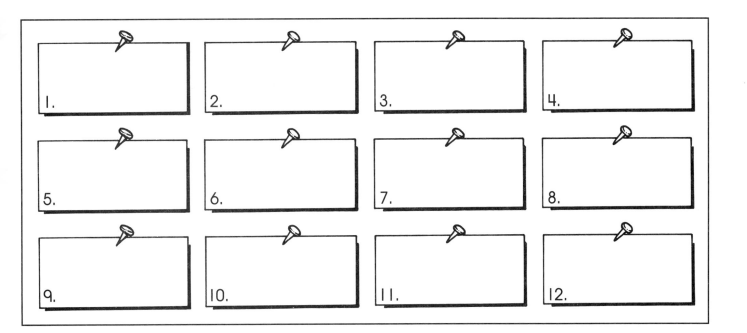

Contractions

An **apostrophe** takes the place of missing letters when two words are combined to make a contraction. Look at the patterns in these contractions.

word + is	she is → she's	he is → he's
word + will	I will → I'll	she will → she'll
word + has	she has → she's	he has → he's
word + are	they are → they're	we are → we're
word + have	they have → they've	we have → we've
word + not	has not → hasn't	did not → didn't
word + would	he would → he'd	they would → they'd

Write a contraction for each pair of words.

1. does not

2. they will

3. you are

4. we would

5. where is

6. had not

7. you have

8. it is

9. he will

10. do not

11. you would

12. could not

Contractions: Review

Rewrite each contraction. Add the apostrophe where it belongs.

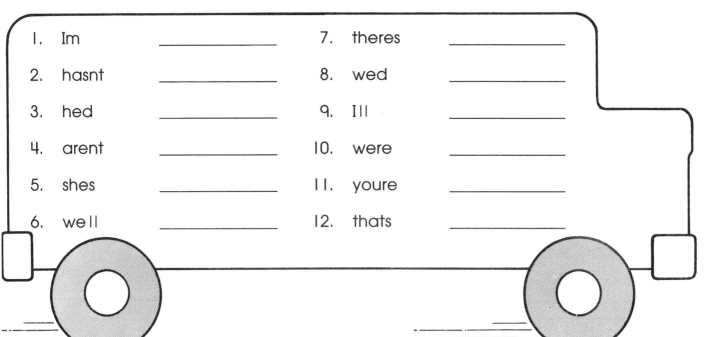

1. Im   _____
2. hasnt   _____
3. hed   _____
4. arent   _____
5. shes   _____
6. well   _____
7. theres   _____
8. wed   _____
9. Ill   _____
10. were   _____
11. youre   _____
12. thats   _____

Write the two words which form each contraction.

13. weren't   _____
14. I've   _____
15. I'll   _____
16. wouldn't   _____
17. here's   _____
18. they're   _____
19. it's   _____
20. shouldn't _____
21. you'll   _____
22. I'd   _____
23. wasn't   _____
24. you've   _____

Contractions: Review

Rewrite each contraction. Add an apostrophe where it belongs.

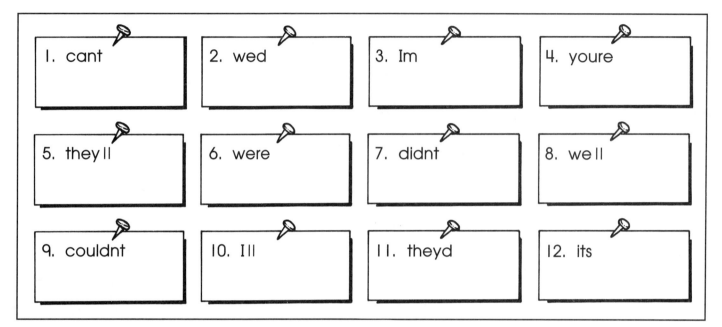

1. cant

2. wed

3. Im

4. youre

5. they ll

6. were

7. didnt

8. we ll

9. couldnt

10. I ll

11. theyd

12. its

Write two words for each contraction.

13. we'll

14. isn't

15. I've

16. that's

17. shouldn't

18. aren't

19. weren't

20. there's

21. you'll

22. I'd

23. wasn't

24. you've

Negative Words

Not, **no**, and **never** are called **negatives**. Do not use a **not** word and a **no** word together in a sentence. **Never** is also a negative word.

right: We never go to bed early.

wrong: We do not never go to bed early.

Circle the correct word.

1. We weren't (never, ever) friends.

2. The music was so loud, we didn't hear (nothing, anything).

3. My dog won't hurt (anybody, nobody).

4. Our team hasn't scored (any, no) runs yet.

5. The child (has, hasn't) done nothing wrong.

6. I haven't (never, ever) used my new camera.

7. I didn't see (no, any) planes landing.

8. Ben (could, couldn't) never finish a large pizza.

9. My cousin hasn't gone (nowhere, anywhere).

10. You (should, shouldn't) never slam the door.

11. Cynthia, (are, aren't) you never going to finish this?

12. I (haven't, have) never been to England.

13. Jayla (is, isn't) never on time for school.

14. There (was, wasn't) never enough snow to ski.

15. Hector didn't (never, ever) forget his mother's birthday.

Negative Words

Circle the correct word.

1. Michelle (could, couldn't) run no faster.

2. I didn't (ever, never) wear braces.

3. My teacher hasn't (none, any) of our grades yet.

4. Kim couldn't drive (no one, anyone) home.

5. Isn't (anybody, nobody) going with me?

6. My family (hasn't, has) no time to travel this year.

7. I don't like to go (nowhere, anywhere) alone.

8. Chris (has, hasn't) done no homework.

9. We (wouldn't, would) never lie to you.

10. Why didn't I get (none, any)?

11. Andrew hasn't (no, any) film for his camera.

12. Diandre, (are, aren't) you never going to finish this?

13. Travis (wasn't, was) saving no money at all.

14. We aren't able to do (any, no) magic tricks.

15. Won't you (never, ever) return my CD?

Write a sentence for each word: **never**, **nothing**, **don't**, and **nobody**.

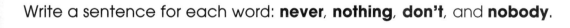

_____

_____

_____

_____

Periods

Use a **period**
- at the end of a statement or command.
    statement—I like to play games.
    command—Wash the dishes.
- after an initial.
    Franklin D. Roosevelt   C. J. Muggs
- after an abbreviation.
    in.—inch   Mon.—Monday   Ave.—Avenue

Place a period where needed.

1. Megan ran one mi on Boise Dr yesterday

2. Mrs Kaplan bought a gal of milk

3. Mr Henry B Lewis is my uncle

4. The Long Co is on McNair St and Second Ave

5. Andrew's ruler is three ft

6. Wed, Sept 3, will be my birthday

7. Lt George S Benally lost 15 lb on his diet

8. Ms Hannson baked a doz cupcakes

9. Waterman Blvd is very wide at Union Ave

10. On Thurs , we will go to St Louis

11. The baby weighed 6 lbs 12 oz at birth

12. Tues , Gov R Hernandez will take office

13. Feb is the month I lost 10 lb on my diet

14. Wood Creations, Inc , is on Main St and Jones Blvd

Commas

Use a **comma**
- between the day and the year in a date.
    November 17, 1955
- between a city and a state.
    Denver, Colorado
- in a series of three or more persons or things.
    apples, oranges, and plums

Place a comma where needed.

1. Kami Reba and Patsy played together.

2. On May 12 2001, we moved to Dallas Texas.

3. The Statue of Liberty is in New York City New York.

4. Grandma and Grandpa were married on June 12 1942.

5. Mia has roses pansies and daisies in her garden.

6. The American flag is red white and blue.

7. I moved from Miami Florida, to Cleveland Ohio.

8. Hawaii became a state on August 21 1959.

9. Tony Gabe Adam and Jerry are my best friends.

10. On Monday Tuesday and Wednesday, it snowed.

11. John F. Kennedy was shot on November 22 1963.

12. We drive through Chicago Illinois, on our way to Madison Wisconsin.

Commas

Use a **comma**
- after the greeting and closing in a friendly letter.

    Dear Nina,   Yours truly, Jason
- to set off a direct quotation from the rest of the sentence.

    Andrew said, "Meet me at 7:00."
- after *Yes* or *No* at the beginning of a sentence or after the name of a person spoken to.

    Yes, I'm feeling better.   Amy, how do you feel?

Place a comma where needed.

1. Chrissie asked "How old are you?"

2. Mother said "I'm going to work."

3. Yes I have finished the dishes.

4. Nikki what TV program are you watching?

5. No I have not finished my homework.

6. Liza where did you go on your vacation?

Place a comma in the letter where needed.

Dear Rachel

    Did you go to Seattle Washington last summer? I went to visit my cousins in Detroit Michigan. When I got home Mom said "Donna did you have fun?"

    I said "Yes it was great."

    Rachel I hope to see you soon.

                                                        Your friend

                                                        Donna

Commas

Use a **comma**
- to separate the day of the month from the year.   (May 3, 1976)
- to separate a city from a state or country.   (Dallas, Texas)
- to set off the name of a person spoken to.   (Brad, come here.)
- after *Yes* or *No* at the beginning of a sentence.   (Yes, I can come.)
- to set words apart in a series.   (I like apples, grapes, and pears.)
- after the first complete thought in a sentence with two thoughts.
     (Hurry up, or we'll be late.)
- after the greeting of a friendly letter and after the closing of every letter.
     (Dear April,   Sincerely, Danny)
- to set off a direct quotation.   ("I'm coming," said Alex.)

Place a comma where needed.

1. My parents were married on March 24 1987.

2. After swimming skating is my favorite sport.

3. I signed my letter "Yours truly Tracy."

4. "Patsy I'll be home late " said Mother.

5. On December 6 1981 Carlos came to America.

6. Exams will be Tuesday Wednesday and Thursday.

7. Sarah missed the bus so she had to walk home.

8. I took my notebook to class but I forgot my pencil.

9. Tyrone asked "Is that a good book?"

10. On the way home I ran into a fence.

11. Yes I bought cereal milk bread and tuna.

12. We went from Miami Florida, to Tulsa Oklahoma.

Apostrophes

Use an **apostrophe**
- in possessive nouns.
    - singular—Tad's record   Shannon's game
    - plural—men's club   bears' tracks
- in contractions.
    - I am—I'm   did not—didn't

Rewrite each underlined word using an apostrophe to show possession.

1. the <u>firefighters</u> boots   _____

2. the <u>trains</u> tracks   _____

3. a <u>ships</u> decks   _____

4. <u>Lynns</u> house   _____

5. several <u>friends</u> games   _____

6. many <u>players</u> uniforms   _____

Write the contraction for each pair of words.

7. he will _____

8. were not _____

9. you are _____

10. we have _____

11. he is _____

12. they are _____

13. It is _____

14. she will _____

Quotation Marks

Use **quotation marks**
- to enclose a direct quotation.

     The teacher said, "Kate, you got 100% on your test."
- around titles of poems, stories, song titles, and reports.

     Trent read "The Owl and the Pussycat."

Quotation marks are placed after the ending punctuation.

Place quotation marks where needed.

1.   Mr. Garcia asked, Daniel, are you going with me?

2.   Grandma read me the story The Rat in the Hat.

3.   The Gift of the Magi is one of my favorite stories.

4.   Are you going to the play? Mona asked.

5.   Anna gave a report called Indians of the Southwest.

6.   My brother can read Spot Goes to School.

7.   Luke remarked, It's very cold today.

8.   Gavin read a report titled Inside the Personal Computer.

9.   Let's get together tomorrow, said Diandre.

10. Have you read the poem called Dancer's Delight in your class?

11. Joey said, Dave, let's play after school.

12. Jenna's report was titled Great Painters.

Name_____

Quotation Marks and Apostrophes: Review

Use **quotation marks**
- to enclose the words of every direct quotation.
    Mandy asked, "What's for lunch?"
- around titles of stories, song titles, poems, and reports.
    I read the poem, "Rip Van Winkle."

Use an **apostrophe**
- to show where letters have been left out of contractions.
    they'll   we're   wouldn't
- to show ownership or possession.
    Donna's shoes   hikers' boots

Place quotation marks and apostrophes where needed.

1. The players equipment was kept in their lockers.

2. Ive finished my report, Famous Athletes.

3. Jennifer replied, Id love to come to your party.

4. My poem, The Beautiful Butterfly, won first prize.

5. Rashads hamsters are frisky.

6. Its Ginnys coat that Sandra is wearing.

7. Arent the boys bikes in the garage?

8. Were doing a report on rockets together.

9. The reporters stories were all too long.

10. My friends birthday is tomorrow.

11. How to Handle Snakes was the title of my report.

12. Julies favorite fish is named Rover.

Punctuation Marks: Review

Place periods, commas, apostrophes, and quotation marks where needed.

1. Our family lives in Memphis Tennessee

2. The boys bicycles were new

3. Ive an uncle named T R Martinez

4. Ms Jung Lola and Becky went to the fair

5. Aunt Heather said I ll be home late tonight

6. Didnt you measure 5 ft last year

7. William asked How much is the candy

8. Mother read us The Very Busy Spider

9. Im going to buy books erasers and pencils

10. Erica were you born on Dec 14 2005

11. Theyre reading The Ships Voyage

12. Sandra please buy a lb of apples

13. Holly said Mom and Dad were married on May 2 1975

14. Shouldnt we read Travel the USA before we leave

15. Were going to Dr Guptas office

16. The three boys sweaters were left in Reid Ohio

17. Ebb Tide is Josephs favorite old song

18. Mr Chu were you in Dallas Texas on May 1 1995

19. Whos going to read the main characters part

20. Vince asked Wheres the fire

Answer Key

Page 5
1. little; 2. near; 3. unhappy; 4. brilliant; 5. wrong; 6. big; 7. present; 8. quick; 9. neat; 10. rock; 11. plump; 12. lift

Page 6
1. under; 2. put; 3. large; 4. robber; 5 over; 6. scared; 7. error; 8. price; 9. sick; 10. small; 11. arrive; 12. talk; 13. reduce; 14. mix

Page 7
1. strong; 2. ancient; 3. cooked; 4. evil; 5. learned; 6. present; 7. sharp; 8. praised; 9. unbolt; 10. assemble; 11. minor; 12. purchase; 13. increase; 14. day; 15. disarray

Page 8
Answers will vary.

Page 9
1. two, to; 2. pear, pair, pare; 3. son, sun; 4. ate, eight; 5. read, red; 6. won, one

Page 10
1. to; 2. tail; 3. knight; 4. sore; 5. waste; 6. steak; 7. beat; 8. wrap; 9. stairs; 10. pause; 11. wait; 12. course; 13. seen; 14. sum; 15. choose; 16. piece; 17. pail; 18. our; 19. aunt; 20. knot

Page 11
1. I would like the whole piece of steak. 2. I'll wear my blue jeans tomorrow. 3. Our mail is not due today. 4. Last night we won four cents. 5. In two days, we go on our cruise. 6. Next week, my aunt might come here. 7. My son will buy new clothes. 8. The new plane that flew by was noisy. 9. You wait right near the gate. 10. I see my dear friend knows you.

Page 12
1. repaint; 2. unfair; 3. incomplete; 4. remount; 5. untouched; 6. rewind; 7. unclear; 8. redo; 9. indirect; 10. unfit; 11. midday

Page 13
1. wonderful; 2. hopeless; 3. graceful; 4. worthless; 5. cleaner; 6. successful; 7. useless; 8. reader; 9. helpless; 10. teacher; 11. cheerful

Page 14
1. meaning (circled), ful (underlined); 2. care (circled), less (underlined); 3. re (underlined), do (circled); 4. fright (circled), ful (underlined); 5. mis (underlined), fortune (circled); 6. garden (circled), er (underlined); 7. pre (underlined), cook(circled); 8. un (underlined), lock (circled); 9. change (circled), able (underlined); 10. pre (underlined), school (circled); 11. wood (circled), en (underlined); 12. mid (underlined), way (circled); 13. in (underlined), active (circled); 14. paint (circled), er (underlined); 15. pay (circled), able (underlined); 16. un (underlined), comfort (circled), able (underlined); 17. wash (circled), able (underlined); 18. pre (underlined), destined (circled); 19. report (circled), er (underlined); 20. fear (circled), less (underlined)

Page 15
1. Dogs; 2. Seven; 3. Apples; 4. Trains; 5. Airplanes; 6. Blue; 7. Pair; 8. Do; 9. Clowns; 10. Snow; 11. Coats; 12. Presents

Page 16
1. Jan Ellen Shaw; 2. Mable Mouse; 3. Paul Mark Conti; 4. Maria Kaylen Foster; 5. Rover; 6. David Joseph Marino; 7. Nadia Lin; 8. Chang Lee; 9. Kenny David Vale; 10. Thad Edgar Taylor; 11. Spot; 12. Jai Ivey Patel; 13. Ebony Grace Freeman; 14. Tabby

Page 17
1. Mr. Jack M. King is my friend. 2. Dr. Robert E. Lewis is my doctor. 3. Mrs. Ana S. Sanchez is my mother. 4. Mia gave me a coloring book. 5. George Washington was our first president. 6. Kahla's dad is Mr. Mario P. Silva. 7. My teacher is Mr. Vincent R. Walker.

Page 18
1. Lisa and Tripp went to see Dr. Stan Young. 2. I live on the corner of Belt Ave. and Boise Dr. 3. My dog's name is Pancake. 4. Did you watch Nick at Nite last night? 5. Mr. Perez works at the Metropolitan Museum. 6. I got presents for Aunt Emily and Uncle Jim. 7. Chandra and I went to the Lincoln Memorial. 8. The St. Louis Cardinals will be in the play-offs.

Page 19
Check placement of months, special days, and holidays on the calendar. 1. January—New Year's Day, Martin Luther King Jr. Day; 2. February—Valentine's Day; 3. March—St. Patrick's Day; 4. April—April Fool's Day, Easter; 5. May—Memorial Day, Mother's Day; 6. June—Flag Day, Father's Day; 7. July—Independence Day; 8. August—Friendship Day; 9. September—Labor Day; 10. October—Columbus Day, United Nations Day; 11. November—Thanksgiving, Veteran's Day; 12. December—Christmas, Hanukkah

Answer Key

Page 20
1. The Mississippi River is east of St. Louis, Missouri.
2. Many Spanish people live in Houston, Texas.
3. Valentine's Day is celebrated February 14.
4. School starts the first Tuesday after Labor Day.
5. I swam in Lake Michigan when I was in Chicago, Illinois. 6. I visited London, England, last July. 7. Hoover Dam and Lake Mead are near Las Vegas. 8. Last Monday, August 17, was my birthday.

Page 21
Positioning of the titles may vary, but they should read: *The Egg and I, Railroads of the World, Cinderella, Cat in the Hat, Jack and the Beanstalk, Goldilocks and the Three Bears, The Story of George Washington, Alice in Wonderland, How to Write Reports, Jokes and Riddles*

Page 22
From left to right: *Alice in Wonderland, Where the Wild Things Are, The Hundred and One Dalmatians, Little House in the Big Woods, Alvin and the Chipmunks, Pink Panther and Sons, Wheel of Fortune, News of the World, The Jungle Book, The Wizard of Oz, The Sound of Music, Charlie and the Chocolate Factory*

Page 23
1. Dad said, "Barry, let's play ball." 2. The teacher asked, "Have you finished your homework?" 3. My note ended, "Your friend, Nina." 4. "That's it," said Sean. "That's the right answer." 5. Mother's note to my teacher began, "Dear Miss Beck." 6. "I got a new bike!" yelled Erik. 7. The thank-you note ended, "Gratefully yours, Mrs. Sabatino." 8. I whispered, "Be quiet, the baby is sleeping."

Page 24
Answers will vary. Check for proper use of capital letters and periods.

Page 25
Circled words: 1. After, Sally; 2. I, *Inside, Personal, Computer;* 3. My, Hudson, School, Forest, Park; 4. Carlos, Spanish, French, English; 5. The, Chung, Terrace, Drive; 6. The, New, Kid, Block; 7. We, *Ghostbusters,* Saturday; 8. Christopher, Columbus, America; 9. I, June, Denver, Colorado, 10. Next, Thursday, Mr., Mrs., Espinosa; 11. My, Harvard, College, Boston; 12. The, Mason, Love, Aunt, Rose; 13. In, Hawaii, Kamehameha, Day, June; 14. Mrs., Friedman, Don't; 15. Stone, Brothers, Hardware, Elm, Street

Page 26
1. S, period; 2. NS; 3. S, period; 4. NS; 5. NS; 6. S, period; 7. S, period; 8. S, period; 9. NS; 10. S, period; 11. NS; 12. S, period

Page 27
1. NS; 2. S, period; 3. S, period; 4. S, period; 5. NS; 6. NS; 7. S, period; 8. NS; 9. NS; 10. S, period; 11. NS; 12. NS; 13. NS; 14. S, period; 15. NS

Page 28
Answers may vary but could include: 1. The little gray squirrel lives in our tree. 2. Bill tied a knot in the string. 3. Each child brought something for the party. 4. The children on my street play kickball. 5. Joanne is a new student this year. 5. My favorite flowers are bright red roses. 6. The dentist gave me a new toothbrush. 7. Our steak was served with brown mushrooms. 8. I took my coat to the cleaners. 9. The lucky ticket had Sierra's name on it.

Page 29
1. S; 2. F; 3. F; 4. S; 5. S; Sentence match: 6. All cactuses have roots close to the top of the sand. 7. Cactuses do not need a lot of water to live. 8. Cactus flowers can be white, yellow, red, or orange. 9. Animals can't eat cactuses because of the spines. 10. The stem of the cactus stores water for dry spells.

Page 30
Answers may vary but could include: I am a nocturnal animal, and I shed my skin. I eat rodents, liards, and even birds. I can inject my poison through my fangs, and I have a rattle at the tip of my tail. It tells me when I may attack. (rattlesnake); I am cold-blooded. My body temperature is the same as the air around me. I am a tiny animal that looks like the giant dinosaurs that lived a long time ago. (lizard)

Page 31
(one line/two lines) 1. The horses/are racing to the finish line. 2. Mrs. Pappas/went to see Jack's teacher. 3. Josh/moved to Atlanta, Georgia. 4. Monica's birthday/is July 15th. 5. The ball/rolled into the street. 6. The policeman/stopped the traffic. 7. Tisha/planned a surprise party. 8. The winning team/received a trophy. 9. The fireworks displays/were fantastic. 10. The heavy rain/drove everyone inside. 11. Adam/looked everywhere for his book. 12. you/Can hear the band outside? 13. Ben and Andre/have just moved here. 14. The whole team/is going to the soccer tournament. 15. My family/has tickets for the football game.

Answer Key

Page 32

(one line/two lines) 1.The telephone call/was for me.
2. Mother/baked a pumpkin pie. 3. Alicia/fed the
baby animals. 4. The Indians/passed the peace
pipe. 5. The garden/needs water to grow. 6. Lisa/has
beautiful long hair. 7. Dion and Ben/played tennis.
8. Our family/went apple picking. 9. The washing
machine/was broken. 10. My grandparents/called
me on my birthday. 11. Alex/bought a new computer
game. 12. We/went on a float trip last summer.
13. My sister/is getting a new car. 14. Brooke/caught
the ball on the first try. 15. Miguel/tried to be first in line.
16. Khalil/earned money for a new bike.

Page 33—34

Answers will vary. Check that each is a complete
sentence.

Page 35

1. Lanky Luke is as tall as the elephants, and Delightful
Denise is as short as her miniature pony. 2. Princess
Penny always wears a party hat, and Prince Pedro
wears a beanie. 3. Fire Hydrant Felipe rides a tiny fire
engine, and his Dalmatian rides with him. 4. Jingles
likes to blow a tin horn, and she likes to throw confetti.

Page 36

1. question, question mark; 2. statement, period;
3. statement, period; 4. statement, period;
5. question, question mark; 6. question, question mark;
7. statement, period; 8. question, question mark;
9. question, question mark; 10. statement, period;
11. question, question mark; 12. statement, period

Page 37

Answers will vary. Check for correct punctuation.

Page 38

1. command, period; 2. exclamation, exclamation
point; 3. command, period; 4. command, period.
5. exclamation, exclamation point; 6. command,
period; 7. exclamation, exclamation point;
8. command, period; 9. exclamation, exclamation
point; 10. command, period; 11. exclamation,
exclamation point; 12. exclamation, exclamation point

Page 39

1. Thurs., Sept. 7, is my birthday. 2. My neighbor works
at J. C. Penney, Inc. 3. Can you run a mile in 15
minutes? 4. Will you take a train to St. Louis? 5. Eat
your dinner. 6. The room measured 25 ft. 4 in. in length.
7. Did Chandra move to Price Dr. last July? 8. Main
St. and 5th Ave. is where Sara lives. 9. Hurry up and
finish that right now. 10. Rev. and Mrs. R. W. Gonzalez
live next door. 11. I bought a dozen apples for Ms.
Ormond. 12. My appointment with Dr. Lee is at 2:30
pm. 13. The baby was born at 6 am and weighed
9 lbs. 13 oz.

Page 40

Answers may vary. Check for correct punctuation:

The Grand Canyon has many trails. These trails
were made by deer, sheep, and the native people of
the region. When the sun sets, the canyon changes
color. How many colors can you see! It is very scary to
look over the edge. The view is beautiful!

On the canyon wall, we saw some Native
American paintings. The designs on the rocks are
called pictographs. They are symbols of objects from
long ago. Have you ever seen a pictograph?

We saw people running the river. Do you know
what running the river is? Climb aboard! It's a chance
to ride the Colorado River on a raft. Wow! You'll get
the ride of your life!

Page 41

1. dog; 2. apples; 3. ice; 4. rainbow; 5. flower; 6. lamp;
7. bus; 8. book; 9. smile; 10. chair; 11. flute;
12. policeman; 13. park

Page 42

1. Carla, Houston, Texas; 2. I, Uncle Chang; 3. *Mister
Ed*; 4. Lincoln Memorial, Washington, D.C.; 5. Aunt
Maria, *Star Wars*; 6. Columbus, America; 7. George
Washington; 8. Fifth Street, New York; 9. Dr. Tony Silva;
10. Yellowstone National Park

Page 43

proper nouns: Snoopy, Ohio, Abe Lincoln, Pacific
Ocean, Peter Pan, Christmas, Monday; common
Nouns: dentist, bear, doctor, school, chief, hotel,
piano

Page 44

proper nouns: Rhode Island, Dr. Ross, Thomas
Jefferson, Jan, New York, Mount Everest, Columbus,
Second Avenue; common nouns: ocean, dog, ice
cream, teacher, park, sheriff

Page 45

1. (one underline) girl, field; (two underlines) deer;
2. (two underlines) squirrels, sides, trees; 3. (one
underline) bunny, bush 4. (two underlines) children,
geese; 5. (two underlines) pictures, books, children,
animals; Sentences will vary.

Answer Key

Page 46
1. cars; 2. pencils; 3. dresses; 4. dishes; 5. birds;
6. sandwiches; 7. sixes; 8. balloons; 9. axes; 10. balls

Page 47
1. bunches; 2. classes; 3. waxes; 4. foxes; 5. brushes;
6. watches; 7. buses; 8. fixes; 9.lights; 10. wishes;
11. passes; 12. switches; 13. dishes; 14. churches;
15. reports; 16. tricks; 17. patches; 18. tickets

Page 48
1. bunnies; 2. mice; 3. men; 4. ponies; 5. teeth; 6. boys;
7. feet; 8. children; 9. cherries; 10. parties; 11. candies;
12. women

Page 49
1. dwarfs; 2. calves; 3. skies; 4. cherries; 5. cuffs;
6. leaves; 7. knives; 8. ladies; 9. armies; 10. roofs;
11. wolves; 12. fairies; 13. lives; 14. halves; 15. shelves;
16. babies; 17. beliefs, 18. loaves

Page 50
1. cod; 2. trout; 3. tuna; 4. geese; 5. elk; 6. men;
7. salmon; 8. oxen; 9. children; 10. women; 11. deer;
12. bass; 13. moose; 14. feet; 15. mice; 16. teeth;
17. pike; 18. sheep

Page 51
fish, houses, boxes, parties, clocks, classes, feet, mice,
lunches, babies, passes, men, ponies, boards, brooms,
wishes

Page 52
From left to right: wishes, hobbies, sheep, days, deer,
bluffs, children, bosses, rashes, cookies, matches,
knives, cars, successes, ponies, feet, kisses, cities,
couches, mice, women, halves, mirrors, trout, persons,
teeth, dresses, girls

Page 53
Answers may vary but could include: 1. dog's; 2. bird's;
3. lion's; 4. flower's; 5. snowman's; 6. dogs'; 7. chairs';
8. firefighter's; 9. cats'; 10. books'

Page 54
1. the children's toys; 2. the monkey's tail; 3. the
animals' cages; 4. the bowlers' balls; 5. my friend's
house; 6. the players' uniforms; 7. Jill's backpack;
8. the runners' shoes; 9. the artist's paintings; 10. the
computer's monitor; 11. the men's hats; 12. my boss's
wife

Page 55
1. Tony's; 2. chickens'; 3. Jonathan's; 4. team's;
5. shoes'; 6. Mrs. Chu's; 7. brother's; 8. neighbors';
9. Ellen's; 10. drivers'; 11. babies'; 12. principal's;
13. bird's; 14. doctors'; 15. painter's

Page 56
1. cats'; 2. Malia's; 3. boys'; 4. Carson's; 5. Avery's;
6. flowers'; 7. bears'; 8. childrens'; 9. sister's;
10. clowns'; 11. Rover's; 12. Miguel's; 13. players';
14. dog's; 15. balloon's

Page 57
Underlined words: 1. washed; 2. took; 3. numbered;
4. need; 5. answered; 6. lost; 7. did; 8. painted; 9. ran;
10. laughed; 11. baked; 12. slipped; 13. thought;
14. Read; 15. looked; 16. ran, jumped; 17. looked, ran;
18. is; 19. are; 20. was, quit

Page 58
Circled words: 1. raced; 2. threw; 3. sped; 4. roared;
5. traveled; 6. went; 11. adored; 12. swam; 13. viewed;
14. divided; 18. sewed; 20. cried; 21. sang; 24. worked;
25. go; 27. paints; Check students' lists of words.

Page 59
Underlined words: hiked, ran, see, find, looked, stood,
scurried, reached, touch, jumped, shouted, watch,
saw, went, slid, stopped, heard, yell; Stories will vary.

Page 60
1. Yes; 2. No; 3. No; 4. Yes; 5. No; 6. No; 7. Yes; 8. No;
9. Yes; 10. Yes

Page 61
1. are; 2. has, is; 3. is; 4. were, went; Stories will vary.

Page 62
Answers will vary. Check for correct use of helping verbs.

Page 63
(two underlines/one underline) 1. might/spend; 2. are/
growing; 3. is/playing; 4. were/going; 5. should/listen;
6. should have/eaten; 7. will/be; 8. can/do; 9. has
been/working; 10. are/going

Page 64
(two underlines/one underline) 1. were/going;
2. have/eaten; 3. must have been/sleeping; 4. are/
going; 5. has/driven; 6. are/playing; 7. was/studying;
8. will be/adding; 9. is/walking; 10. am/planning;
11. have/gotten; 12. may be/riding; 13. should be/
coming; 14. have been/cutting

Page 65
(two underlines/one underline) 1. Have/seen; 2. did/
tell; 3. am/working; 4. has/gone; 5. is/going swimming;
6. should/chew; 7. can/get; 8. Did/marry; 9. have/
been; 10. might/finish; 11. Does/start; 12. can/play;
13. (one underline) was; 14. (one underline) am;
15. have/been; 16. has/been; 17. can/finish; 18. (one
underline) is

Answer Key

Page 66
Underlined words: 1. was; 2. has been watering; 3. has gone; 4. stood; 5. has eaten; 6. are; 7. have collected; 8. will keep; 9. Read; Circled words: 10. were; 11. are; 12. is; 13. was; 14. has been; 15. am; 16. were; 17. are

Page 67
From left to right: buries, waxes, washes, bites, speaks, likes, catches, measures, bosses; 1. shaves; 2. sings; 3. taste; 4. teaches; 5. dashes; 6. fly; 7. crosses; 8. play; 9. wait; 10. make

Page 68
1. studied; 2. baked; 3. smelled; 4. washed; 5. smiled; 6, grabbed; 7. copied; 8. trimmed; 9. named; 10. spied; 11. melted; 12. clipped; 13. toasted; 14. popped; 15. emptied; 16. played

Page 69
From left to right: smiled, chopped, grabbed, studied, hopped, loved, stepped, supplied, smelled, planted, copied, flipped

Page 70
1–14. Answers will vary. Check for correct use of verbs, helping verbs, and endings.

Page 71
1. ate; 2. took; 3. went; 4. seen; 5. given; 6. gone; 7. saw; 8. took

Page 72
Answers may vary but could include: 1. First, Aunt Betty picked out the paint for the shutters. 2. Then, Aunt Bety and Jenny shopped for food for the picnic. 3. Next, they stopped to get gas for the car. 4. After they shopped, Aunt Betty asked Jenny to wash the car. 5. Finally, Aunt Betty's sisters arrived to have dinner.

Page 73
1. ate; 2. came; 3. given; 4. drove; 5. did; 6. come; 7. broken; 8. driven; 9. eaten; 10. broke; 11. did; 12. given; 13. gave

Page 74
1. fell; 2. took; 3. ran; 4. broke; 5. knew; 6. began; 7. threw; 8. ate; 9. slept; 10. shone; 11. brought; 12. began

Page 75
1. ran; 2. gone; 3. saw; 4. threw; 5. run; 6. written; 7. took; 8. seen; 9. grew; 10. went; 11. taken; 12. thrown; 13. thrown; 14. gone

Page 76
From left to right: tasted, fried, fixed, knotted, ended, voted, raised, stopped, rubbed; 1. eaten; 2. seen; 3. took; 4. went; 5. done; 6. given; 7. ate; 8. taken; 9. saw; 10. gone

Page 77
Circled in order of occurrence: will walk, will go, will make or squawk, will growl and roar, will eat, will pick, will join, will, will share; Paragraphs will vary. Check for correct use of future tense.

Page 78
1. (underlined, future tense) are, will (the pyramids) be; 2. (underlined) look, will look; 3. (underlined) find, will find; 4. (underlined) visit, will visit; 5. (underlined) study, will study; 6. (underlined) compares, will compare; 7. (underlined) write, will write; 8. (underlined) donates, will donate; 9. publishes, will publish; 10. receives, will receive

Page 79
1. This afternoon, I will pick up groceries at the store. 2. I will call the painter to paint the shutters. 3. The neighborhood will build a float for the parade next Friday. 4. The picnic lunch at City Hall will be tomorrow. 5. Jenny will come on Thursday. 6. The violin quartet will play on Saturday.

Page 80
1. her; 2. us; 3. you; 4. him; 5. They; 6. them; 7. I; 8. We; 9. me; 10. He

Page 81
1. I; 2. We; 3. us; 4. He; 5. them; 6. You; 7. him; 8. me; 9. her; 10. he

Page 82
1. it, they, them; 2. it, they; 3. they, it, he or she; 4. It, they; 5. He or She, it; 6. them; 7. them, it

Page 83
In order of occurrence: penguins, air, air sacs, penguins, wings, wings, cold water, nest, eggs, male, eggs, eggs, skin flap, babies, babies, babies

Page 84
1. This house is his. 2. Her friends came for dinner. 3. Their school is large. 4. That bicycle is mine. 5. This game is yours. 6. Pancake is his.

Page 85
1. your; 2. his; 3. his; 4. Its; 5. our; 6. My; 7. yours; 8. Her; 9. Our

Answer Key

Page 86
(Circled in order of occurrence) They, us, her, me, I, them, their, them, they, I, they, they, them, me, his, she, her, you, my, I, them, me, their, their; Finished stories will vary. Check for six circled pronouns.

Page 87—91
Answers will vary. Check for correct use of adjectives.

Page 92
1. softer; 2. longest; 3. smaller; 4. lowest; 5. warmest; 6. sweeter; 7. coldest; 8. taller; 9. neater; 10. fastest; 11. shortest; 12. older; 13. smaller; 14. largest

Page 93
1. easy, easier, easiest; 2. brave, braver, bravest; 3. scary, scarier, scariest; 4. red, redder, reddest; 5. nice, nicer, nicest; 6. hungry, hungrier, hungriest; 7. blue, bluer, bluest; 8. noisy, noisier, noisiest; 9. flat, flatter, flattest; 10. fast, faster, fastest

Page 94
1. most useful; 2. cleaner; 3. scariest; 4. more talented; 5. taller; 6. most delicious; 7. funnier; 8. neatest; 9. most unusual; 10. biggest

Page 95
1. worst; 2. worse; 3. best; 4. good; 5. best; 6. worst; 7. better; 8. bad; 9. better; 10. worse; 11. best; 12. worst

Page 96
(underlined adjective/circled noun) 1. new blue/car; 2. this/winter, (underlined) cold, (underlined) icy; 3. furry/cat, my back/porch; 4. brave/firefighters, small/children; 5. My/parents, new/table, lamp; 6. Many/birds, large/bird feeder; 7. American, red, white, blue/flag; 8. one/brother, two/sisters; 9. sharp/knife, tough/meat; 10. handsome/man, beautiful/woman; 11. mysterious/spaceship, dense/forest; 12. chocolate/cupcakes, large/plate; 13. longest/race, one/hour; 14. tennis/shoes; 15. young/children, sandy/beach; 16. Ten/clowns, tiny/car; 17. little, black/kitten; 18. six/bibs, tiny/nephew; 19. Many/people, big/race, last/Saturday; 20. funniest/act, two, crazy/clowns

Page 97
(underlined) 1. behind; 2. with; 3. outside; 4. in; 5. next; 6. up; 7. inside; 8. around; 9. off; 10. under

Page 98
(circled/underlined) 1. at/the whistle's blow; 2. by/a woman, in/a purple dress and hat; 3. for/my ticket; 4. to/the club car, for/lunch; 5. For/lunch, 6. After/lunch, to/Littleville; 7. in/the purple dress; 8. by/the window; 9. of/the trip; 10. At/three, in/the afternoon, in/Littleville

Page 99
1. quietly; 2. yesterday; 3. inside; 4. carefully; 5. upstairs; 6. tomorrow; 7. slowly; 8. neatly; 9. outside; Book: 1. How; 2. When; 3. Where; 4. How; 5. Where; 6. When; 7. How; 8. How; 9. Where

Page 100
1. how, when, where; 2. how, how, how; 3. where, where, where; 4. how, when, where; 5. where, how, when; 6. how, when, when; 7. how, where, when

Page 101
Answers will vary. Check for proper use of adverbs.

Page 102
1. good; 2. well; 3. surely; 4. really; 5. real; 6. well; 7. well; 8. surely

Page 103
(circled verb/underlined adverb) 1. got/early; 2. cleaned/slowly; 3. rides/often; 4. walked/cautiously; 5. washed/today; 6. started/Suddenly; 7. took/outside; 8. used/carefully; 9. went/early; 10. slid/safely; 11. got/happily; 12. came/again; 13. helped/Earlier; 14. fought/bravely; 15. finished/quickly; 16. baked/Yesterday; 17. takes/upstairs; 18. gets/monthly; 19. threw/everywhere; 20. crept/quietly

Page 104
1. We/P, feed/V, birds/N, regularly/Adv; 2. Derek/N, planted/V, maple/Adj, tree/N, yesterday/Adv; 3. Chang/N, wrote/V, them/P, letter/N; 4. They/P, have/V, two/Adj, small/Adj, dogs/N; 5. Ruby/N, will be dancing/V, tomorrow/Adv; 6. toys/N, were/V, everywhere/Adv; 7. three/Adj, children/N, are going swimming/V, today/Adv; 8. You/P, can eat/V, now/Adv; 9. They/P, washed/V, car/N, carefully/Adv; 10. Several/Adj, thirsty/Adj, children/N, drank/V, cold/Adj, lemonade/N; 11. We/P, run/V, three/Adj, miles/N, often/Adv; 12. chorus/N, has been singing/V, beautifully/Adv; 13. He/P, gave/V, Chris/N, five/Adj, dollars/N; 14. Paige/N, washed/V, dishes/N, slowly/Adv; 15. That/Adj, tiny/Adj, baby/N, was sleeping/V, soundly/Adv

Page 105
1. an; 2. a; 3. a; 4. an; 5. a; 6. an; 7. an; 8. a; 9. an; 10. a; 11. an; 12. a; 13. An; 14. an

Answer Key

Page 106
1. an; 2. a; 3. An, a; 4. a; 5. an, a; 6. an; 7. a, an; 8. an; 9. an; 10. An, a; 11. an, an; 12. a, an; 13. an, a; 14. an, a; 15. An

Page 107
1. isn't; 2. she's; 3. they've; 4. he's; 5. I'd; 6. you're; 7. she'll; 8. didn't; 9. he'll; 10. where's; 11. they'd; 12. she's

Page 108
1. doesn't; 2. they'll; 3. you're; 4. we'd; 5. where's; 6. hadn't; 7. you've; 8. it's; 9. he'll; 10. don't; 11. you'd; 12. couldn't

Page 109
1. I'm; 2. hasn't; 3. he'd; 4. aren't; 5. she's; 6. we'll; 7. there's; 8. we'd; 9. I'll; 10. we're; 11. you're; 12. that's; 13. were not; 14. I have; 15. I will; 16. would not; 17. here is; 18. they are; 19. it is; 20. should not; 21. you will; 22. I would; 23. was not; 24. you have

Page 110
1. can't; 2. we'd; 3. I'm; 4. you're; 5. they'll; 6. we're; 7. didn't; 8. we'll; 9. couldn't; 10. I'll; 11. they'd; 12. it's; 13. we will; 14. is not; 15. I have; 16. that is; 17. should not; 18. are not; 19. were not; 20. there is; 21. you will; 22. I would; 23. was not; 24. you have

Page 111
1. ever; 2. anything; 3. anybody; 4. any; 5. has; 6. ever; 7. any; 8. could; 9. anywhere; 10. should; 11. are; 12. have; 13. is; 14. was; 15. ever

Page 112
1. could; 2. ever; 3. any; 4. anyone; 5. anybody; 6. has; 7. anywhere; 8. has; 9. would; 10. any; 11. any; 12. are; 13. was; 14. any; 15. ever; Sentences will vary.

Page 113
1. Megan ran one mi. on Boise Dr. yesterday. 2. Mrs. Kaplan bought a gal. of milk. 3. Mr. Henry B. Lewis is my uncle. 4. The Long Co. is on McNair St. and Second Ave. 5. Andrew's ruler is three ft. 6. Wed., Sept. 3rd, will be my birthday. 7. Lt. George S. Benally lost 15 lbs. on his diet. 8. Ms. Hansson baked a doz. cupcakes. 9. Waterman Blvd. is very wide at Union Ave. 10. On Thurs. we will go to St. Louis. 11. The baby weighed 6 lbs. 12 oz. at birth. 12. Tues., Gov. R. Hernandes will take office. 13. Feb. is the month I lost 10 lbs. on my diet. 14. Wood Creations, Inc., is on Main St. and Jones Blvd.

Page 114
1. Kami, Reba, and Patsy played together. 2. On May 12, 2001, we moved to Dallas, Texas. 3. The Statue of Liberty is in New York City, New York. 4. Grandma and Grandpa were married on June 12, 1942. 5. Mia has roses, pansies, and daisies in her garden. 6. The American flag is red, white, and blue. 7. I moved from Miami, Florida, to Cleveland, Ohio. 8. Hawaii became a state on August 21, 1959. 9. Tony, Gabe, Adam, and Jerry are my best friends. 10. On Monday, Tuesday, and Wednesday, it snowed. 11. John F. Kennedy was shot on November 22, 1963. 12. We drive through Chicago, Illinois, on our way to Madison, Wisconsin.

Page 115
1. Chrissie asked, "How old are you?" 2. Mother said, "I'm going to work." 3. Yes, I have finished the dishes. 4. Nikki, what TV program are you watching? 5. No, I have not finished my homework. 6. Liza, where did you go on your vacation? Letter: Dear Rachel, Did you go to Seattle, Washington, last summer? I went to visit my cousins in Detroit, Michigan. When I got home, Mom said, "Donna, did you have fun?" I said, "Yes, it was great." Rachel, I hope to see you soon. Your friend, Donna

Page 116
1. My parents were married on March 24, 1987. 2. After swimming, skating is my favorite sport. 3. I signed my letter, Yours truly, Tracy. 4. "Patsy, I'll be home late," said Mother. 5. On December 6, 1981, Carlos came to America. 6. Exams will be Tuesday, Wednesday, and Thursday. 7. Sarah missed the bus, so she had to walk home. 8. I took my notebook to class, but I forgot my pencil. 9. Tyrone asked, "Is that a good book?" 10. On the way home, I ran into a fence. 11. Yes, I bought cereal, milk, bread, and tuna. 12. We went from Miami, Florida, to Tulsa, Oklahoma.

Page 117
1. firefighter's; 2. train's or trains'; 3. ship's; 4. Lynn's; 5. friends'; 6. players'; 7. he'll; 8. weren't; 9. you're; 10. we've; 11. he's; 12. they're; 13. It's; 14. she'll

Page 118
1. Mr. Garcia asked, "Daniel, are you going with me?" 2. Grandma read me the story "The Rat in the Hat." 3. "The Gift of the Magi" is one of my favorite stories. 4. "Are you going to the play?" Mona asked. 5. Anna gave a report called "Indians of the Southwest." 6. My brother can read "Spot Goes to School." 7. Luke remarked, "It's very cold today." 8. Gavin read a report titled "Inside the Personal Computer." 9. "Let's get together tomorrow," said Diandre. 10. Have you read the poem called "Dancer's Delight?" 11. Joey said, "Dave, let's play after school." 12. Jenna's report was titled "Great Painters."

Answer Key

Page 119

1. The players' equipment was kept in their lockers.
2. I've finished my report, "Famous Athletes."
3. Jennifer replied, "I'd love to come to your party."
4. My poem, "The Beautiful Butterfly," won first prize.
5. Rashad's hamsters are frisky. 6. It's Ginny's coat that Sandra is wearing. 7. Aren't the boys' bikes in the garage? 8. We're doing a report on rockets together.
9. The reporters' stories were all too long.
10. My friend's birthday is tomorrow. 11. "How to Handle Snakes" was the title of my report. 12. Julie's favorite fish is named Rover.

Page 120

1. Our family lives in Memphis, Tennessee. 2. The boys' bicycles were new. 3. I've an uncle named T. R. Martinez. 4. Ms. Jung, Lola, and Becky went to the fair. 5. Aunt Heather said, "I'll be home late tonight." 6. Didn't you measure 5 ft. last year? 7. William asked, "How much is the candy?" 8. Mother read us "The Very Busy Spider." 9. I'm going to buy books, erasers, and pencils. 10. Erica, were you born on Dec. 14, 2005? 11. They're reading "The Ship's Voyage." 12. Sandra, please buy a lb. of apples. 13. Holly said, "Mom and Dad were married on May 2, 1975." 14. Shouldn't we read "Travel the USA" before we leave? 15. We're going to Dr. Gupta's office. 16. The three boys' sweaters were left in Reid, Ohio. 17. "Ebb Tide" is Joseph's favorite old song. 18. Mr. Chu, were you in Dallas, Texas, on May 1, 1995? 19. Who's going to read the main character's part? 20. Vince asked, "Where's the fire?"

Notes